At Powerline & Diamond Hill

Unexpected Intersections *of* Life and Work

At Powerline & Diamond Hill

Unexpected Intersections of Life and Work

Lee Snyder

Foreword by
Jeff Gundy

DreamSeeker Books
TELFORD, PENNSYLVANIA

an imprint of
Cascadia Publishing House

Cascadia Publishing House orders, information, reprint permissions:
contact@CascadiaPublishingHouse.com
1-215-723-9125
126 Klingerman Road, Telford PA 18969
www.CascadiaPublishingHouse.com

At Powerline and Diamond Hill
Copyright © 2010 by Cascadia Publishing House LLC
Telford, PA 18969
All rights reserved
DreamSeeker Books is an imprint of Cascadia Publishing House LLC
Library of Congress Catalog Number: 2009053839
ISBN 13: 978-1-931038-74-4; **ISBN 10:** 1-931038-74-0
Book design by Cascadia Publishing House
Cover design by Gwen M. Stamm
Cover art: based on a detail from "Grandmother and the Coburgs," by Kathryn
Holman Moore, courtesy of Lee Snyder, owner of the painting.

The paper used in this publication is recycled and meets the
minimum requirements of American National Standard for Information Sciences—
Permanence of Paper for Printed Library Materials, ANSI Z39.48-1984.1984

See cre   ge for prior publications this book excerpts or adapts as well as for
notations on Bible versions used.

Library of Congress Cataloguing-in-Publication Data
Snyder, Lee.
   At Powerline and Diamond Hill : unexpected intersections of life and work /
Lee Snyder ; foreword by Jeff Gundy.
      p. cm.
   Summary: "How does a Mennonite farm girl, whose 'closed' Oregon commu-
nity prescribed a limited role for women and distrusted education, end up a uni-
versity president? The author explores the paths that opened her doors to education and leadership"--Provided by publisher.
   Includes bibliographical references.
   ISBN-13: 978-1-931038-74-4 (5.5 x 8.5" trade pbk. : alk. paper)
   ISBN-10: 1-931038-74-0 (5.5 x 8.5" trade pbk. : alk. paper)
   1. Snyder, Lee. 2. Snyder, Lee--Childhood and youth. 3. Mennonites--Ore-
gon--Harrisburg--Biography. 4. Community life--Oregon--Harrisburg--His-
tory. 5. Women college presidents--Ohio--Bluffton--Biography. 6. College
presidents--Ohio--Bluffton--Biography. 7. Bluffton University (Bluffton,
Ohio)--Presidents--Biography. 8. Women--Education--United States--Case
studies. 9. Leadership in women--United States--Case studies. 10. Harrisburg
(Or.)--Biography. I. Title.
   CT275.S5873A3 2010
   289.7092--dc22
   [B]

                                                            2009053839

            17 16 15 14 13 12 11 10   10 9 8 7 6 5 4 3 2 1

For Del, with love and gratitude

Contents

Foreword:
What's Another Word for "Rebel"?

A few years ago I invited faculty and staff to sit in on the first "spiritual memoir" class I taught at Bluffton. Of the half-dozen who took me up on it, the most faithful was the Bluffton president at the time, Lee Snyder. Unlike the rest of us, Lee never complained about how busy she was and never blew off a class unless she was out of town. She would simply settle in near the back of the room, and perhaps talk a bit to students nearby. Once we began, she generally said little, though she listened closely and recorded what went on in her small notebook. When I asked the class to choose a favorite quote from the reading, she always found something good—often she had read farther into the book than others had managed to get—and something astute to say about it.

Lee wrote some closely observed, beautifully balanced, and deeply reflective essays that semester. If memory serves me, some of that writing is to be found in the book you are holding, though in substantially different form. But the remarkable thing about Lee's writing, like her presence in our class, is its freedom from ego and special pleading. Far from expecting special treatment because she was The President, she simply behaved as though she were just one of the group—and so truly became one of the group. Most Mennonites (as someone pointed out to me long ago) are very bad at accepting praise, but when someone complimented her work, Lee would just smile graciously, nod, and then turn the subject to something else.

When the class ended, if I remember correctly, I told her that I hoped the work she had done would turn up in print somewhere, but she was noncommittal—again, typically. So I am very grateful that now we have *At Powerline and Diamond Hill.*

Early in this vivid and subtly revealing memoir, Lee Snyder reflects on her conservative Mennonite community in Oregon this way:

> While I never actually rebelled against the community's strict expectations, rituals, and beliefs, I gradually began to see that the sharp lines of separation and supposedly clear boundaries were much murkier than anyone wanted to admit.

Now wait, I thought when I first read this passage: a young woman leaves her community to become a leader at two Mennonite universities and the first female president at any of them, earns a Ph.D. in English, and takes on churchwide leadership roles—this isn't a rebellion?

Perhaps this is one secret of Lee Snyder's success: she made her most dramatic moves in such an unassuming, unaffected way that they seem far less radical than they were. Throughout this memoir we see Lee (with husband and partner Del) taking one bold step after another as opportunities to serve and to lead present themselves. Her account of answering the phone while folding laundry one Saturday represents, in my mind, a proto-typical Lee Snyder moment:

> I finally had the good sense to excuse myself and shut off the washer, learning only later that this was not a call from just the board chair and the head of the Bluffton presidential search committee but that a number of other committee members were listening in as well. Later, folding towels and matching socks, I found the routines of the laundry a near perfect way to focus the mad scramble of questions as I thought about Ed's call.

There is no politicized refusal of "women's work" here, but neither is there a glib or easy acceptance of gender roles. Among the many fascinations of this book is its complex, experiential analysis of feminism. Snyder later quotes her mother's question, "Will you have a good man to work for?" with wry humor, but reflects seriously on the tension implicit in her situation:

> that of a faith community committed to hierarchical roles and also to a belief that individuals are called out for God's purposes—sometimes against the grain of embedded religious and cultural strictures. The tension could be wrenching, but it was life-giving also as I matured in my understanding of what God might be asking me to do.

This luminous book, full of lively stories of what God has asked of Lee Snyder and astute reflections on the life that she has lived in response, makes for fascinating and instructive reading. It is one more generous gift from Lee to the Mennonite community and the wider world.

—*Jeff Gundy*
Bluffton University

Author's Preface

". . . to arrive where we started and to know the place for the first time." —T. S. Eliot

When I was a child listening in on adult debates, often about controversial church issues, I believed that when I grew up I would know the answers. Where this stubborn conviction came from is hard to imagine, since there always seemed to be unsettled and perplexing matters constantly worrying the grownups. Eventually I would find consolation in accepting, as someone has said, that "living is a form of not being sure." This account is really an exploration of many questions, but one which bows down to the mystery of the ordinary yielding to the extraordinary. How does a farm girl, whose parents had little opportunity for education and whose community proscribed a very limited role for women and distrusted education, end up a university president?

This was not a matter of career or vocation. Growing up in a Mennonite family, I did not know women who had career goals. I never had any. Instead, I have been overtaken by other questions regarding providence, destiny, calling, luck, fortuities and convergences. I am still surprised by the glimpses every now and then of how these forces call us out of and beyond ourselves.

I also discovered through the writing how important remembering is in creating the self, as I considered the strange twists and turns of a life which is both unremarkable and unexpected. Memory takes on a life of its own, weaving threads of connection between knowing and not knowing. Remembering that childhood ache of uncertainty and the desperate desire to have things settled, to *know,* is a memory more precious than painful. I would eventually figure out that lives are shaped not only by how we pursue the future but by how we consolidate fragments of the past; by what we remember and what we forget; by the stories we are told and by the stories we tell.

It is necessary to recognize at the outset that memory is not reliable or that, as Czeslaw Milosz concludes, "The past is inaccurate." All memories are partial, selective, and shimmer through the refractions of time, the mind's balkiness and the soul's defenses. In remembering the past, particularly childhood events, I have attempted to be truthful to the power of memory as well as respectful of the facts. I have taken some liberties in the narrative of imagining the backdrop of times and places, attempting to reassemble reasonable particulars that would enlighten the question of why a certain memory has such a hold on me. But I have to concede, as W. S. Di Piero has observed, that to some extent "remembering is an act of the imagination."

This story, which begins with a place—a farm and a church—represents a personal journey of discovery; an attempt to uncover those pivotal forces which are never fully understood in constructing a life. At the same time, I take responsibility for the shape of the story, acknowledging that this is more about a search than a recounting of simple facts. Extended family members would no doubt have their own version of the "facts," and their variations might very well be more accurate.

What I know is that a particular fact rarely stands on its own; it is seen through the prism of a many-faceted reality; it depends on point of view. This is made startlingly clear when in family conversations, for example, we discover that our older daughter remembers a particular childhood incident very differently than the younger, prompting good-humored teasing about what could have created such a skewed memory. And, while childhood memories are family affairs, I am convinced that they serve as private negotiations on the way to becoming a self.

Thus this account represents one particular storyline, with a very few names and locations changed to respect individual privacy. My hope in telling this story is that I will honor those who have loved me and have taught me. Finally, this is not simply an account of the past but rather the tracing of a trajectory which reaches into unknown territory, which stretches toward the future. At the center of it all is the timeless present worked out through everyday rhythms of hunger and fullness, of sun and wind and rain, of light and darkness, of inexorable and unreasoned joy, of discontent and gratitude.

—*Lee Snyder*
  Harrisonburg, Virginia

PART ONE

PLACE

Knowing One's Place

"Why would you want to do this?" I was startled by the question. It was an unseasonably cold night in early November 1995. It had not occurred to me to bring a winter coat. My husband and I found our way to the designated lounge, waiting to be summoned for a reception at which I would be introduced as the presidential candidate. "Why would you want to do this?"

It was a good question, one which at the time I could not have answered adequately. This stately, elegant trustee wife, who also was waiting for the trustees to finish their session and for the candidate reception to follow, was gracious but direct. She sized me up, wondering why a woman would want such a job. Or more to the point, what audacity had brought me to Bluffton? I do not remember what I said; I must have stammered, searching for the polite response. How much did I reveal about my own uncertainties? For the truth is that I was not sure I did want the job.

But this is getting ahead of the story. It all starts with a place—and the year a five-year-old meets God personally. For one growing up in the 1940s and early 1950s on a ryegrass farm in a close-knit Mennonite community, God was the main thing. Even before being aware of myself, really, I had developed a private and personal sense of God as the center of the universe—not only in the prescribed rituals of church and home but through the raw splendor of a life dependent on planting and harvest, on rain and sun, on dirt and fertility.

It was a place of abundance but also of tragic losses. I cannot remember when I first learned that I had been named after my father's seven-year-old sister who died of diphtheria. I knew the names of my twin brothers almost as soon as I knew my own name. To a two-year old, Donald and Ronald were there but not there. My mother's private grieving for these babies born too soon was revealed only by a recitation, when I would ask, of just the bare facts: Donald lived two and a half hours and Ronald lived three. Over the years, when I would return to the valley to visit my parents, the short story of my twin brothers' lives was extended by afternoon or evening walks down to the Alford Cemetery, where my mother and I visited the simple grave stones there in the shadow of the tall cedar next to the great-grandparents.

Where God was in all this, including my teen-age cousin's accident while helping his grandfather with the harvest, was not clear. When he got his legs caught in the combine augur, we could not bear to imagine those amputated limbs. But, in general, circumstances were—well—just what they were.

Loss was cushioned by an unshakable and unquestioning faith structured into daily routines. Our lives were ordered by nightly Scripture reading, while prayer at meal times dispensed a thrice-daily dose of gratitude. To ravenous children, these prayers were interminably long. They seemed purposely extended when the telephone happened to ring while our heads were bowed and my father refused to be hurried. For us kids sitting around that chrome table in the dining room, we waited to see which would happen first—the caller giving up or Dad ending his prayer in time for one of us to make a mad dash to the phone before it stopped ringing.

But meeting God personally was another matter. Looking back, there is the indelibly etched image of a particular day, a child weighed down by the intensity of a private encounter. Is this a real memory or a collage of images which have taken on a life of their own? Walking home from school, head bent into the wind, shivering in a thin blue coat, the child is hardly aware of the dead sky or the pelting sleet as she prays. As she treks down the road toward the farmhouse, the dormant fields are folded into the awful silence. Even the girl's shoes make no sound against the wet gravel of the pavement. With a child's unmitigated belief, absorbed from the life of the church community, this girl knows that God is real and means what he says.

This was my first crisis of faith, I now realize, and a marker along the way toward discovering my place in the God-scheme. I was six. My most prized possession was a maroon Gideon New Testament. One day I lost it. I was devastated. When it did not turn up after much searching, I began praying that God would give it back. My prayers became pleading, demanding. "Please God. Please God."

How many days did these relentless prayers go on? Did my mother become concerned when I asked four, five, or six times a day where else we could look? I imagine Dad obliging me when I thought of yet another place to check, down behind the seat cushions of the Chevy.

Even after Mom and Dad had exhausted every possibility in helping me search for the New Testament, I hung on to a grim hope that my prayer would be answered. Going to bed, buried in one of the family quilts, I tried to think of ways God might respond. I knew that God, so choosing, could simply open up the heavens, reach down, and return the New Testament. It was as simple as that. There was the story from Sunday school where God meets Moses but allows Moses only to see God's back. Maybe God would allow me to see his hand reaching down out of the clouds, handing me the Testament?

My prayers continued for days, with a fierce insistence and an unwavering belief that God would intervene and honor his promise, "Ask and you shall receive." While my parents knew how much I wanted my Bible back, I have no idea if they sensed the desperate drama going on between their oldest child and God. What would Heaven do with a six-year old who believed literally that God was going to give back the Testament?

God gave it back.

While the details remain hazy, it must have happened something like this: One evening a car pulled up into the driveway. A man got out and knocked on the door. From way on the other side of town, Mr. Edwards showed up at the door. "I brought something I think your little girl must have left at our place the other week when you stopped in. We found this after you left." In his hand, Mr. Edwards held out the maroon Testament. "I was just driving over this way anyway, and the wife thought your daughter might want this back."

I did not even hear my father thank Mr. Edwards. It was not until Dad had closed the front door that I could move.

"Here you are," Dad said. "I knew it would turn up."

Mom, hearing the commotion, came in from the kitchen, drying her hands on her apron. "Where did that come from?" looking first at Dad then at me.

"Mr. Edwards dropped it off. We left it at their new house when we went over to see their house plans."

All Mom said was, "I had no idea you took your Bible along."

She went back to clean up the kitchen. Dad took up his reading. The household settled back to normal.

While that experience appears to an adult as embarrassingly naïve, I have no doubt that God answered my prayer. It was as though the heavens had opened and God had handed back my Testament.

That child-God encounter was one marker along the way of discovering one's place—a place in the God-scheme of things. Finding one's place, both literally and figuratively, reaches toward the ineffable and yields glimpses of both the imagined and the not yet in our consciousness. That place is where we start from.

Grandmother and the Coburgs

An unexpected university encounter much later proved far more significant than what began as simply a walk through the student union. This was 1972. After a ten-year stop-out, I was back in college to finish my Bachelor's degree, interrupted by marriage at age nineteen to my high school sweetheart. Then it was beginning a family and a service term in West Africa for three years. One day, I headed into a walk-through gallery at the University of Oregon student union, with a few minutes between classes. I surveyed the exhibit of Oregon artists. I was irresistibly drawn to a large painting. It was called "Grandmother and the Coburgs."

I could not have explained the impact of what I was seeing. Though somewhat abstract, the representation was a scene I knew immediately. I knew the Coburg Hills at the south end of the valley as one approached Eugene. There was the familiar cluster of cottonwoods and a little building perched up on the hillside. I was transfixed by the nearly hidden figure in the painting—the profile of a blue face cut off at the very top of the frame, strands of long hair transmuted into wispy curtains of rain blowing across the ridges. The more I looked at the painting, the more I recognized—for this was a view of the mountain familiar from our farm up the valley. I could not have explained exactly what I was feeling and seeing beyond the multi-variant greens, deep reds and oranges, the contrasts of pale yellow and brilliant turquoise, the depths of light and dark.

What William Stafford once said about poems describes what happened to me that day: "'There is something about it that won't yield to ordinary learning. When a poem [painting] catches you, it overwhelms, it surprises, it shakes you up. And often you can't provide any usual explanation for its powers.'"

I know now that the power of this painting for me was in the gathering up into some connected whole a range of only dimly perceived understandings—about what it means to be a child of the West, about the pervasive influence of ancestors, about the breathtaking and ever-changing beauty of the valley and the mountains with their female forms both hidden and revealed—all of this and more. It was about color and texture and the sweep of heights. It was about the mystery of place inscribed in that inscrutable face only half revealed on the canvas, signaling some epiphany I did not comprehend. I simply had to find Del, my husband and best friend, and show him the painting, the first time a piece of art had ever moved me in this way.

"Grandmother and the Coburgs" (for me it would have been perhaps grandfather rather than grandmother) summoned unarticulated questions and tapped into some submerged reality regarding identity, heritage, and tradition. Even though my world was circumscribed by the wisdom of fathers in church and home, my mother is not irrelevant in this story, because she surveyed those same mountains through her kitchen window. There she kept track of the ever-changing Cascades, in turn fierce or ravishingly beautiful, depending on the weather. I call my mother the "keeper of the weather." Always attuned to the ordinary practicalities of the everyday, my mother knew that the well-being of our family was dependent on favorable weather conditions for the crops.

There is a postscript to the story of "Grandmother and the Coburgs." As students, Del and I knew what it meant to be poor. I desperately wanted the painting but could not imagine finding the dollars for the gallery price. A friend knowledgeable about the workings of the art scene suggested that I make an offer to purchase the painting after the exhibit closed. He assured me that would not offend the artist, and I could tell her how much I liked her work.

I tracked down the artist's address and wrote to Kathy Moore, who lived in Eugene. I was still only dimly aware of the reasons I had been so moved by "Grandmother and the Coburgs," but I tried to express how the painting had drawn me. I sent off the letter but received no reply. It was disappointing, but there was some comfort in the fact that we had been saved from an extravagance we could ill afford. Weeks later, amid final projects and papers, the artist called to say that she had received my letter and would have accepted my offer to buy the painting, but that she had already sold it. By that time I had made my peace with the fact that I could not have the painting.

The day I completed my last courses for an undergraduate degree in English Literature, I walked into our little house on Tyler Street and there was "Grandmother and the Coburgs" hanging on the wall—indescribably beautiful, with the added mystery of how Del had negotiated the purchase. To this day he will not disclose whether or not he paid the gallery price. What I do know is that the painting pulled me toward home and some deeper, if unarticulated, understanding of myself.

A sense of place determines who we are, I suspect, maybe even who we will become. If we are lucky, we will discover home, although that is a lifetime exploration. Through six moves over the next years, from West Coast to East Coast and then to the Midwest and back to Virginia, "Grandmother and the Coburgs" has been carefully packed up with the household belongings. It reminds me of who I am.

✠

At the Corner of Powerline and Diamond Hill Roads

Place also shapes an understanding of destiny. In my case, gaining a sense of what it meant to be a westerner came slowly, overshadowed by the more pressing expectations of being part of a close and closed religious community. I have come to know that as a daughter of forebears who forged their place in a green valley which promised prosperity and possibility, I was singularly blessed. Above all, the ethic of hard work and commitment to the Mennonite faith defined the center for my father and grandfather and great grandfather—a place as real as any location in Lane County, Oregon, where they settled. Heading west offered a stake in the future which appealed to these entrepreneurs.

I return always in my mind to the plain white church which sits conspicuously among the ryegrass and fescue fields at the corner of Powerline Road and Diamond Hill Road. Surrounded by a gravel parking lot, the church house presents itself as solitary and set apart, except on Sundays or on midweek prayer meeting nights when the Chevrolets and Fords, interspersed with a few Buicks, drive in. This place pulls the farmers from their fields even amid harvest. Whatever the season, the church guards and guides the rhythm of work and worship for its members.

Eventually I would become aware of the inexplicable, and for some suffocating, power of the church to circumscribe the life of the community and its individual members. For Powerline Road, which connected to Highway 99E and intersected the Southern Pacific Railroad running by my parents' farm, not only brought the folks to the church; it also took them away.

Having taken that road myself, I discovered that leaving was not a simple matter. In a recurring dream, I would be back at the church there at the intersection of Powerline and Diamond Hill roads. For years, in this nightmare I would be the outsider, showing up without the required woman's prayer veil or the proper clothes. But I kept going back until, in these dreams, I again belonged in the congregation where the men still sat on one side of the sanctuary and the women and girls on the other.

Belonging was a part of the geography of the place, protected in that valley by abundance, by community, by fellowship, and by the surrounding mountains. Heading out Diamond Hill Road to the two-room school house, then on to the foothills, one finally arrives at the valley rim, the immovable purple Cascades. Sometimes draped in rain and fog, those mountains loomed large in our psyches, strong and masculine in their craggy shapes, but at places softened by light and the contours of the secondary hills that nestled at the lower elevations. As a child, I was particularly fascinated by the big bear outlined on top of the mountain, a shape created by the peculiar cutting of the giant Douglas firs on the high ridge.

Meandering through our farm was Little Muddy Creek, fringed by ancient oaks, providing endless childhood adventures. I loved the sound and feel of whispery dust which poofed when we stepped on the oak puff balls. I learned patience and persistence when fishing with safety pin hooks for the gray crawdads which lurked along the banks. And to a four or five year old, daring to walk across the precarious foot log was a test in courage, incubating a fear of heights which still plagues me.

The creek which threaded through the uncles' and grandparents' and cousins' farms, flowed by the church, but figured most prominently in our everyday lives—in the imaginations of the children or in the complications for the farmers and dairymen who had to contend with flooding or drought. "The creek's up," my dad would announce. Usually that raised no alarm, for this was just a part of the natural ebb and flow of things. But sometimes it was inconvenient if not dangerous. The oft-repeated story of the big flood when my sister was born, and the difficulties of getting the doctor, underscored the necessity of living with forces over which we had no control.

Growing up, I lived in two worlds, both sacred and endlessly fascinating. Life on a farm was an enclosed world, in many ways. Drenched in rain and sun by turns, we took for granted the emerald grass fields and the golden crops. The bounty of valley fruits, some growing wild by the road to be picked for berry cobbler, and the blessing of a strong harvest yield were gratefully received.

In the other world, the church, the preachers offered God their puny lives and thanked him for salvation. When the crops were dismal, when the rains came at the wrong time and wrecked the promise of a good yield, or when the price for the seed fell to new lows, the Mennonite farming community stubbornly thanked God for his goodness and hoped for better times. *Arbeit and Hofe*, work and hope, the Mennonite martyrs' credo, shaped this Oregon community of Mennonite settlers, some of whom came still speaking German. They took seriously the biblical command of nonconformity and separation from the world, and always they took themselves seriously. Sometimes too seriously.

It was the promise of the seasons, the ever new cycles of planting and harvest, the reassurance of the rains and mysteries shrouded in the fog-warmed valley, that softened the proscriptions of the preachers who presided over the rules and regulations for the Mennonites. Strictures against radios, flashy cars, immodest dress, and anything worldly, from Christmas trees to professional sports, applied generally to the community.

But the most burdensome expectations were imposed on the women and girls who were instructed to be subject to husbands and fathers, every day enacting a God-given hierarchy by covering their heads and not cutting their hair. First Corinthians 11 was a Scripture known by every woman young and old in the congregation, a powerful directive which kept women in their place.

Then there was the day we "received baptism," as the preachers described it. Contrary to usual practice, boys and girls sat together at the front of the church. This was a once or twice a year ritual when the youth of the congregation who had declared a commitment to faith at the spring or fall revival meeting became members of the church. To make a "decision for Christ" was the only way to be freed from the waves of guilt induced by the fiery preachers who issued graphic warnings about the judgment awaiting those who resisted salvation. That I can still remember the names of those circuit evangelists, James Bucher, C. F. Derstine, Andrew Jantzi, and George R. Brunk II, confirms their marvelous power. That I can still recall the ecstasy that I felt the night I raised my hand in response to the preacher's "invitation" should not surprise me, but it does. We sang "O Happy Day," and I was truly happy.

What stands out from that baptismal morning was not the undercurrent of joy or even that sense of being on edge as we entered what was in fact the most significant initiation rite of the community. Kneeling, we bowed our heads as the deacon poured water into the bishop's cupped hands where he stood in front of each of us by turn. Bishop John, reciting the sacred words, turned his hands outward letting the water flow onto our heads.

We had prepared ourselves for the cold shock, for the wetness spreading on shirts and dresses. What we had not thought much about was the Holy Kiss. At least the girls were not prepared. The conclusion to the baptismal sacrament was "the extended hand of fellowship," whereby we were each raised off our knees with a handshake and each received the ceremonial Holy Kiss. Gentle Bishop John reached out his farm-calloused hands and greeted each of the boys while the bishop's wife did the same for the girls. The rough whiskery kiss of Mrs. Yoder so took us aback that we forgot our damp hair.

✛

Contradictions—Insiders and Outsiders

As the first daughter of an up-and-coming young farmer, I was nurtured by a healthy sense of place—my place in a closed community of believers—and by a rootedness in the natural world which included the vastness of the Pacific, evergreen forests and the spring planting. One world was restrictive, the other mostly life-giving and wondrous. Only as I entered adolescence would I begin to glimpse the contradictions inherent in these vastly different but inextricably linked spheres.

Living in the Harrisburg community, I understood myself to be an *insider,* defined in opposition to the label given our Catholic and Protestant neighbors who were all *outsiders.* In daily interactions, the Cersovskis, the Grimes, the Bowers, the Langdons, the Hustons, and the Estergards were part of the respected and familiar cast of characters in work and school. They were *other* and did not have equal footing with the Hostetlers, Kropfs, Yoders, Millers, Neuschwanders, and Smuckers. I grew up with a sense of being special, of being part of a faith tradition obedient to a higher call.

That sense of being special was bolstered by my first-grade teacher, Mrs. White, who saw me as a quick learner. I understand now that it was not so much that I was an unusually talented student as it was that Gladys White had the gift of making a child feel special and eager to achieve, to understand the sweet pleasure of learning for its own sake.

But the lessons were not always sweet. I was in elementary school. It was Saturday, a chance to read after the cleaning chores were done. Sometimes I could snatch a few minutes between dusting and vacuuming. The telephone rang. Mom answered as usual. "Yes, Mrs. Goldsworthy?" My teacher. It must be about the refreshments the children were to bring for the party. There was a long pause, a loud silence, as Mom stood there at the phone. She was staring out the window toward the railroad tracks just beyond the near rye grass field. There was nothing on the tracks. They were just there, empty, awaiting the next freight train. What was this about? As a nine or ten year old, I was suddenly scared.

Overhearing this one-sided conversation, I examined my life. What had I done? My teacher often told me to slow down. Had I hurried too much? "Try to be a little neater with your writing," she would say. Here I was a failure, both in my impatience and in a lack of natural ability to master the gorgeous sweeps and flourishes of the Palmer method of penmanship. Mrs. Goldsworthy was a good teacher, giving herself generously to her four grades—half the students in the two-room country school. Although she was not a part of the Mennonite church, she had old-fashioned values which satisfied the Catholics, the Baptists, the Methodists, and the Mennonites.

From the next room, I strained to hear all I could, because this had to be about school. Maybe Mrs. Goldsworthy had been more angry than she had let on when the day before she had had to warn me twice—no—three times to stop talking. There was not a clue in the silence as Mom stood there in the dining room with the receiver in her hand. I remember a clutch of fear, of some creeping danger.

Then my mother said, "I will talk to her." Mom put down the telephone and stood in the doorway.

I closed my book, waiting. My mother had the strangest look on her face that I had ever seen. It was not anger. It was worse. She stood there as though paralyzed, color drained from her face. Now I was afraid, not for myself but for her. I wanted to go over and tell her it was all right.

I fingered the rough cloth of the old couch, tracing the pilled nylon fibers, and I picked at the snag at the edge of the cushion. We both heard the eleven o'clock train whistle as it approached our crossing. Duke barked outside.

Mom still looked funny. "Mrs. Goldworthy. . . ." She started, then trailed off. The old chime clock on the mantel began ticking loudly. Mom smoothed her apron. Now she looked like herself again. "That was Mrs. Goldsworthy," she said. "She told me that Mrs. Evers had stopped in to talk with her yesterday after school. Charlotte was feeling very badly that you and your friends were talking about her family. What did you say?"

The Evers. Not once had Charlotte Evers crossed my mind in those moments of soul-searching. Now I felt sick. I knew what I had said, that I had repeated to my best friend and other girls at recess what I had overheard Mom and Dad discussing. I had betrayed my parents and hurt my mother. I knew what guilt was, but this was hard to sort out. I thought about blond Charlotte, one of the new kids who arrived in the middle of the year when her parents moved into the old rundown house several miles up Powerline Road. They were outsiders with a capital O. Anyone driving by their place could not help but notice the old furniture or an appliance or two on the porches and a generally unkempt yard. Low-class renters was the unspoken judgment of these upstanding Mennonites. Charlotte and her sickly little brother came to school with clothes which were always clean but in need of mending.

For weeks the community had buzzed with the news of another break-in. First, there was the shop broken into on the road into town. Then there was a report of another burglary somewhere. The community was outraged. Next one of the families had returned from church to find that their house had been burglarized while they were gone. Rumors began to circulate that it must be someone who had at least some knowledge of the comings and goings of this sedate Mennonite community.

Talk was that Charlotte's older brothers had come home because they had not found decent work elsewhere. Being the only newcomers to the area, it was only too easy to make them the target of the gossip over the recent burglaries. The Evers moved around, it seemed, and clearly the boys were unreliable and shiftless. Who had started the rumor was not known. But the speculation about the Ever boys was the story I had heard from the grownups and carried to school. Now Mrs. Goldworthy had told my mom that Charlotte said I had been spreading lies about their family.

I looked at Mom, expecting the worst. At the very least, I expected a scolding and instructions that I must make an apology to Charlotte. Instead Mom just turned, suggesting that I finish dusting. She headed for the laundry room. That was it. I was neither blamed nor absolved.

I sometimes wonder how much of that day I actually remember. The truth is that I do not recall all the details, just the ghastly feeling that I had done something unforgivable. Looking back, I know now that on the day Mrs. Goldworthy called my mother, I understood for the first time something about the pain we inflict on others in our arrogance and self-righteousness as a religious community. Developing empathy for the *outsider* was key to understanding myself. The sense of guilt in a nine-year old can be terrible and terrifying. That Saturday is still painfully raw in my memory. I was learning something about the contradictions and tensions inherent in seeking one's place—as an insider or an outsider—or both.

In a complicated way, my Uncle Elwyn was searching for his place too, and I knew that and worried about him with the anxieties of a nine- or ten-year-old. My mom's youngest brother, Elwyn, only a few years older than me, was fun. I had only a child's sense that Elwyn and his next older brother Danny were in trouble with the church authorities. I began including these two handsome uncles in my nightly prayers, that God would save them from hell.

Whether it was smoking, running around with town girls, or going to movies, Elwyn's flirting with what the preachers would have called "the world" burdened my deaf grandparents, who themselves knew what it meant to be *outsiders*. They did not quite fit in the church, and they were certainly outsiders in most social circles. Elwyn had to get away. He sought freedom by joining the navy.

As younger nieces, we loved our uncle for his dash and daring. I still treasure the romantic studio photo of him dressed in his sailor whites. Defying the Mennonite belief in not going to war, Elwyn effectively turned his back on the church by joining the armed services. And the church turned its back on him. As a pre-teen, I understood that this was a soul struggle. I had a dogged conviction that if I prayed hard enough and did not give up Elwyn would return to the faith.

Even after he committed suicide years later, I still prayed for him—and for myself. The call came in early January. I was now a college dean in Virginia, keeping in touch with family through letters, phone calls, and periodic visits to Oregon. My mother was utterly stricken by her younger brother's death. "They found him in the garage," she told me, feeling it necessary to provide the details. "He shot himself."

I tried to comfort my mother over the phone, telling her that Elwyn was not himself. A brain tumor, unbearable pain, and desperation had to be taken into account. I still pray for Elwyn, for love and forgiveness. And I pray that the church at the corner of Powerline Road and Diamond Hill Road may be forgiven as well.

✠

Words and "the Word"

Scripture was the centerpiece of everything the church stood for. The Word, as expounded literally by the preachers on Sunday morning or as dramatized in our Sunday school lessons, was the foundation of our daily lives. The Bible's God-man-woman hierarchy, with angels somewhere in there, ordered our lives. The men were the keepers of women's souls. Humility, order, and simplicity were virtues lifted high in our world. Work was on the list too: work, humility, order, and simplicity.

While the Word was the guiding principle of our lives, *word*, with a small "w," was also honored at home. My father indulged a passion for books, for reading of any kind. Invariably he had a book or periodical in his hand when he was not out in the field or working in the warehouse. Stacked next to his easy chair, on a shelf just below his Bible and Sunday school lesson guide, was a pile of *Farm Journals*, the *National Geographic,* and information on health matters. There were fundamentalist and church periodicals as well as reports of miracle healings in charismatic circles, and there was foreign mission news.

I can only conclude that Dad's eclectic and voracious reading habits made up for his lack of formal education. All six of us children had access to Dad's extensive library in what we called the "den," just off the living room. While the theological materials were for the most part beyond us, the books on end-time prophecies with their astonishing time charts and diagrams of beasts and other apocalyptic features drew us in. Of even more interest than the occasional biography was the odd publication on flying saucers, a particular interest of my dad's.

A classy set of the *Encyclopedia Britannica*, with gold-embossed spines, occupied a prominent place in the study, lined up on the beautifully grained wood bookshelf made just for these enormously heavy volumes. This luxury purchase from a traveling salesman must have provided a rather sharp contrast to the otherwise utilitarian and modest furnishings of the living room and study. Surrounded by implement calendars or Scripture mottos on the wall, I cannot say much about our family's aesthetic sensibilities—but in books and reading materials I had access to what were actually vast resources.

For me, reading of all kinds became a way to escape a constricted and sometimes stifling world. Sitting up under the rafters in our dim, hot attic going through back issues of the *National Geographic,* I was lured by the exploration of exotic places. This was my introduction to Greek and Egyptian mythologies, to strange African cultures and to the breathtaking beauty of the world of beasts and insects, rainforests and savannahs. To those of us reared in an environment in which modesty was viewed as next to godliness, the *National Geographic* offered an education in the human body as well, from the photos of naked tribal women to the voluptuous nudes of the art world.

After my father died, when my mother was dismantling his library and moving to a retirement home, I discovered among Dad's things a 1917 copy of the *Seven Laws of Teaching,* by John Milton Gregory, First Regent of the University of Illinois. While education was always suspect in our church circle, here was confirmation—at least so I convinced myself—that my father would have approved of my own vocation in academe, that he honored formal education. Every so often I take out that small, yellowed volume with its ordered and practical approach: the laws of teaching, of the teacher, of the learner, of the language, of the lesson, of the teaching process, of the learning process, of review and application. I take it out to reconnect with my father who taught me to love learning.

✛

Aunt Daisy

I admit it, I inherited my father's insatiable curiosity as well as his eclectic reading habits. But it is to a strange great aunt that I owe my love of literature, as well as an emerging sense of the complexities of status—of *insiders* versus *outsiders*. Aunt Daisy's private indulgence was reading novels. She passed them around. My cousins and I were the recipients of her Elsie Dinsmore books—a series of Civil War historical novels of dubious literary merit. Daisy was another one of those in our Mennonite community who experienced the conflicting identity of insider and outsider. She was one of a number in my mother's extended Hostetler family who was deaf.

These "deaf and dumb" relatives, as they would have been described in those times, found sweethearts and marriage partners outside the community, often at state schools for the deaf. I ache to know more about my great-grandmother, Elsie Hammontree, and what she gave up when she left her entire family and moved from Missouri to Oregon, marrying fellow deaf student Joseph Hostetler. My grandmother Viola fell in love at deaf school with Oscar Stewart, a playful and loving man who somehow managed not to take the church too seriously. Where Aunt Daisy found Willy, a wizened and odd little man, is one of those mysteries the family narrative has not explained.

What remains indelibly impressed on my memories of that community, however, is that the church welcomed these outsiders—deaf persons outside the mainstream—and those who chose to join the church through marriage. The Harrisburg congregation made room at the back of the sanctuary, reserving a section of the wood benches just for the deaf attending Sunday services. The sermon and hymns were interpreted by one of the hearing family members. Even a church like ours could make allowances. The men and women in the deaf section did not need to sit separately; they could share the same benches.

It was through Aunt Daisy's books that I entered another world entirely. While I never actually rebelled against the community's strict expectations, rituals, and beliefs, I gradually began to see that the sharp lines of separation and supposedly clear boundaries were much murkier than anyone wanted to admit. I also began to understand what books meant for Daisy. I shall always be grateful that she found entry into imaginative worlds and shared novels with her great nieces.

I have sometimes wondered how she got by with this, given the suspicion of anything worldly by our conservative community. But for some reason, my parents did not raise questions about our reading. We had full access to the school library and later to a little town library. Fantasy, adventure, romance—the *Arabian Nights a*nd the classic fairy tales—drew me. They provided a counterpoint to my father's books and periodicals. Daisy's taste for fiction and her generosity in sharing her books hooked me. She would hand-pick particular Elsie Dinsmore volumes for individual nieces. There must have been twenty or thirty in the series. Aunt Daisy would stick a scrap of paper with our name written out in a spidery cursive in the particular book selected just for us.

We cousins borrowed each other's books so we could keep up with the unfolding story of several generations in the Civil War south. I got my first introduction to at least some version of that history, including the horrific cost to families of the war, vivid accounts of the activities of the Ku Klux Klan, and some understanding of the Reconstruction and Carpetbagger era. But what really attracted me were the traumas and tribulations of the heroine I identified with, a girl who struggled constantly to be obedient. She could never be good enough to please her father, and this caused her considerable anguish.

An oldest daughter, I too never could be good enough. I always seemed to be naughty, to sass my mom, to fight with my sister, to have my head in a book when I was supposed to be working. We kids were loud and scrappy. I recall the anxiety I would experience as we headed home from Sunday night or Wednesday evening church, my sister and I in the back seat of our black Chevy waiting for Dad's verdict—were we going to get a spanking when we got home because we had misbehaved in church? Curiously, I remember virtually nothing about the actual spankings. Mostly I remember the dread.

✛

Intimations

While I lost myself in books, our home brought other outside influences as well. Much of my mother's creativity was expressed through her cooking and gardening, her flowers, and her quilts. These were housewifely pursuits sanctioned by those defining a woman's place. My mother found her own way to conform yet to invite outside interests and influence. She was generous and known for her hospitality. A warm, outgoing person, she managed an efficient household and made entertaining guests seem easy. Her welcome of the stranger, the neighbor, the vast network of relatives, or the new family in church found endless expression in bountiful meals and in sharing produce from her garden.

Each Saturday, she would bake pies or some other dessert planning to invite someone home for dinner after church. There seemed always to be an assortment of fascinating people around our table. There were foreign missionaries and churchmen who especially interested my dad. I loved to eavesdrop on their conversations. There was the neighbor dairy man who stopped in to play checkers with my dad in fall or winter on slow days. There was Ben Vimont, who seemed a larger-than-life character to us kids, a mix of health-food nut and religious fanatic. He was passionate, you had to say that for him; a curmudgeon who seemed a holdover from frontier days. He was welcomed in our home whenever he would pull up in his rattle-trap VW bus.

With always a soft spot for the single men in the church who were widowed or whose wife had run off, Mom would invite them for Sunday dinner. The names Paul or Chester or Tim or Floyd or Elmer run like a litany through any recitation of my parents' gestures of hospitality. We children were not always kind, barely able to hold in laughter when Chester, a bent old man with a long wispy beard, would repeat a story again and again, circling back after a few bites of roast beef and peas to what we had just heard minutes before. Even my mom saw the humor in this, acknowledging his senility. She also understood the deprivation of a man who had lived for years in a near hovel up the road, raising a son who was partly daft—whether from genetic misfortune or from the lack of a mother's love, was not clear.

My mother believed in feeding "the least of these," as Jesus Christ taught us. There was always good food, even for the occasional hobo who walked up to our house from the railroad tracks which bordered the farm. In winter, the hobos went south to warmer climates. Reversing in the spring and summer, the vagrant traffic up through the Willamette Valley increased. It was another Saturday. Dad was in town trying to get a tire patched. My mother was late finishing her pies because an Illinois friend had stopped in unexpectedly. The children were down at the creek fishing. I can imagine the irrational clutch of fear Mom must have felt as she looked out the kitchen window and saw the hobo headed up the road. She would have watched as he turned into the drive. I can see her, putting a floured hand to her chest as the stranger approached. Duke began to bark. Then the chained German Shepherd growled, which only heightened the sense of danger.

This is the story I tell myself, trying to imagine whether, in my mother's bounded and circumspect life, that particular hobo visit was welcome or unwelcome. Then the front doorbell rang. He would not dare come around the back, for fear of the dog. The doorbell rang again. Should she ignore it? What if the man discovered she was home alone?

A third time the doorbell sounded. He would not leave, my mother realized. She also knew that the front door was not locked—it was never locked, in fact. Back in the kitchen she quickly wiped her hands on the dish rag, steadied the rolling pin, and smoothed back her hair. Opening the front door, she saw a young, swarthy man standing there, startlingly handsome. She imagined that she caught a whiff of whiskey on his breath. He had obviously not shaved for several days, and she guessed that his clothes had come from the Salvation Army. She stood there at a loss. Normally it was "Come on in," to the neighbors who stopped by, though they usually came to the back door. The stranger peered around her. She sensed that he was sizing things up, concluding that she was alone.

"Would you be able to spare some food?" He broke the silence. "I am on my way to Portland to see my mother, and I knew this would be a good place to get a meal." Later she would tell the family, "I finally pulled myself together and asked him to go round to the picnic table in the back." Now she was wondering, "How did he know our place would be a good place for a meal?"

"Yes, I'll get you some food," she told him. "Just come around to the back where you can eat in the shade. The dog is chained; he won't bother you." As soon as the man turned to follow her directions, she shut the front door and twisted the knob to lock it. Back in the kitchen, she surveyed the leftovers in the refrigerator. She wanted to prepare a respectable meal. There was cheese, fruit, sometimes pudding, and always garden produce on hand. Her dilemma today was how to fix a good meal quickly, so as not to prolong his stay.

The two remaining pieces of fried chicken from last night and the leftover mashed potatoes and gravy were obvious choices. These could be heated while she set out homemade cottage cheese, a brand new batch she had prepared for Sunday's company dinner. As the skillet sizzled and the gravy softened from its solid state to a mixture of lumps and sauce, she took three slices of bread from the loaf, added a plate of margarine and the summer's wild blackberry jam to a tray. *Oh yes, he might want apple butter for the cottage cheese,* she thought.

Through the window, she saw the man out back, eyeing the dog. *Why doesn't he sit down at the picnic table?* she wondered.

Grabbing a handful of carrots and celery from the crisper, adding a glass of milk to the tray and collecting the cutlery, she was ready. By the time she took these out the chicken would be hot, the mashed potatoes warmed, and the gravy steaming. Her appearance seemed to reassure the visitor, and he sat down as she set the table. "I'm bringing the hot food," she announced, heading back to the kitchen.

How did he choose our place? Feeling safer now that the dinner was nearly ready, the man's comment still nagged at her. She dished up the potatoes, arranged the drumstick and chicken breast alongside, and poured the gravy into a small server. With both hands full, she pushed the back door open with her foot and hurried out. "Thank you," he said, giving her a respectful, appreciative look.

"I'll bring you some dessert—cherry cobbler," she said as the man began to eat. Back at the kitchen window, she could not take her eyes off his back. The half-rolled pie crust lay on the counter, drying out in the heat. A fly settled on the handle of the flour sifter. The small back burner glowed red hot where she had heated the gravy. She imagined the man's mother in Portland but told herself that the hobo's story was just to gain her sympathy. He was handsome, she had to admit, if one disregarded the stubble on his chin and his unkempt clothes. His hair was curly, his hands finely shaped. She could picture them spooning out the cottage cheese, holding the drumstick.

She was staring—what she always scolded the children about. She saw him reach for the last piece of bread, carefully spreading it with jam, then folding the slice and eating it like a sandwich. Maybe she had not given him enough? Two pieces of chicken were not much for a hungry man. She would be generous with the cobbler and add some ice cream.

Watching him, she saw him swipe up what must have been the last bit of gravy with the bread crust. Even with his back turned, she imagined what she could not actually see. Then he put both hands down at his sides, resting them on the wooden bench. He did not turn around nor look at the dog. By now Duke was quiet, simply getting up every so often to turn around and move a little further into the shade.

It was time to take out the dessert. Setting down the bowl of cherry cobbler and ice cream, my mother saw he had eaten all the food. Before she knew what she was saying, she asked, "How did you know that you would get good food here?"

He looked up, as surprised as she was at the question. He turned his head and pointed up toward the railroad, just visible through the walnut grove on the other side of the garden. "There are a series of telephone poles next to the tracks, just below the crossing there, marked with two big chalked Xs," he said. "One X means a good meal, but two means that the food is extraordinary." Looking back at her, he added, "And I am not disappointed. You are a good cook. This is the best meal I have had in a week."

She wanted to ask him more. Where had he come from? Where had he stopped? Did he always travel on freight cars, jumping from line to line as the hobos did when they crossed from east to west or from south to north? She imagined that he wanted to tell her. But there were no words that could pass between this plain woman and the traveler. Only food and drink were permissible. Perhaps for a brief moment, this woman was overcome with an irresistible urge to throw off her apron, to abandon the baking, to leave the kitchen in a mess, and to set off on some unimagined adventure. Then the dog barked, the stranger started, and the voices of the children could be heard coming up the lane from the creek.

The summer sun was hot again. "It's just the children," she explained as the man looked warily at the dog straining against the chain. The children entered the farm yard, stopping short at the sight of the hobo sitting at the picnic table talking to their mother. These mysterious figures always evoked curiosity and just a twinge of fear. The tramps were both welcome and not welcome, an ambiguous status conferred on all outsiders, but especially on these suspicious characters who were fed and hurried along.

Embarrassed by the children's staring, their mother instructed them to go on in the house and clean up. She picked up the dishes and followed. "Thank you," he called after her as he stood up, wiped his mouth and headed out the lane. Just at that moment, Dad drove in with the pickup. "Who was that I just met?" he asked. "Another hobo? It seems like we have had had more than usual, lately."

"He told me why," my mother said, and explained the peculiar food rating system on the rail route. It seemed to all of us that there was something different about this hobo visit, but we would not have been able to say what. It is clear to me now that I have filled in some of the blanks trying to make sense of my mother's life. I have wondered why certain childhood memories stand out, why they rouse themselves from the back reaches of our minds and take on a life of their own. Someone has described this recall of family stories, of anecdotes—real and embellished—these threads of history, as weaving "lies and lives together." A way we figure out our own relationship to ourselves, to each other and to God.

Here we were, a group of Mennonites who were curiosities in the broader community, embracing with a fierce religious fervor some of the same commitments that characterized those who had come west to find whatever it was they were seeking: opportunity, life purpose, exploration of new things, freedom from some indefinable cultural or family or social burden. Being a child of the West has meant many things, including a certain sense of destiny and calling nurtured by the religious community in which I grew up. That this could include an overture to the stranger, a welcome to persons from far places, was an enormous gift that saved not only our parents from a pinched and constricted life but nudged us children to seek broader horizons.

Even something as insignificant as play times could be an exploration of boundaries, something I realize only in retrospect. I remember playing office. Sure, along with cousins and friends, we played school, we played church, we played ball and we found wonderful hiding places in the haymow. We girls pretended to can pickles using our mothers' empty Mason jars, filling them with green and yellowing cucumbers that remained in the garden at the end of the summer. We played "house," reinforcing the prescribed roles we were taught—dads doing their jobs and moms cooking, cleaning, and taking care of the babies.

But my father's papers stacked on his desk encouraged a fascination with "the office." As an eight-year-old, I salvaged Dad's discards from the waste basket: letters and bulletins, reports and statements. Whatever mailings ended up in the trash could be mine. I can still see my dad's desk against the north wall of the study, just off the living room. Fastened to the wall above the desk was the head of a deer with deep amber eyes of glass, its nose unnaturally shiny. One of my father's hunting trophies, this specimen carried a large rack of antlers that nearly touched the ceiling.

There on what was commonly called a "knee hole desk," Dad organized the fertilizer bills, tax forms, contribution requests, investment reports, and the sundry papers which he wanted to review further. With his books near at hand in the glassed-in wall case, Dad shared the study with my mom on those days she opened the Singer sewing machine under the south window to mend torn shirts or to sew a new dress for one of her four daughters. I could spread out my "office" materials in whatever corner of the living room or den that I chose. It was a solitary occupation. I wonder now if my younger sisters simply had no interest or if I needed my own private diversions?

PART TWO

FORTUITIES

✛

Fortuities and Convergences

It began as an ordinary evening in Portland, Oregon, the kind of evening which beckons the future. A time and space in which God shows up incognito. This is really my husband's story, but it has become mine as well. That afternoon, Del came home from his Madison High day in the classroom and reported that the math department head had gotten sick and had invited Del to take his place at a dinner that night honoring Oregon math students. Del went to the event and found himself seated next to Professor Meier from the University of Oregon, who Del knew from previous studies in Eugene.

We had recently returned from a teaching stint in West Africa. It so happened that Professor Meier's Lutheran uncle was in Nigeria at the same time we were, and we had met him on an occasion or two. So Del and Gene Meier, over salad and roast chicken, made a connection at dinner that night. When Del came home, he told me of the coincidence of meeting up with Gene Meier and of the discovery of the Nigeria link. Del reported, almost as an afterthought, that Professor Meier knew of some National Science Foundation (NSF) money available at the university. He had encouraged Del to apply if he wanted to continue graduate studies.

That math dinner was to have enormous consequence for our family. Del was granted an NSF award. In 1969, we left Portland and returned to Eugene, locating where our two daughters were within walking distance of their elementary school. Del continued his math studies and, at age twenty-eight, I decided it was time to finish college. Actually, Del decided it was high time I get back to the classroom if our family were to avoid any number of foolish projects and schemes that, to escape boredom, I had begun thinking about. After all, there is only so much cooking and cleaning a stay-at-home mom can do.

There is something incredible about how weighty that particular evening turned out to be based on a such a flimsy succession of developments—the department head getting sick in the first place; Del a last minute invitee, then being seated next to a former professor—who just happened to be there; finally the encouragement of Dr. Meier to apply for funds that he personally had some control over and that were still available for math and science teachers.

I could not have known then that this move would virtually change my life. But first it was negotiating reentry into university after stopping out for nearly ten years. Cautious counselors suggested taking a lighter course load, advice I ignored. But, I admit, I was terrified. Could I do the work? Could I compete in the classroom? Even finding my way around a vast, unfamiliar campus added to the anxiety. Registration, with long lines and closed classes, seemed a daunting obstacle. Del led me through the maze which wound in and around McArthur Court. There we sought out the English department table amid the History, Comparative Literature, and Humanities setups; got the proper stamps and signatures; and were able to confirm financial aid arrangements. Del walked me around to the assigned classrooms so I could get my bearings, so I could figure out where Fenton Hall or Deady or Prince Lucien Campbell was situated.

By now I had decided on English, not an easy choice since I also had a fascination for biology. Literature or science? That was the question. In high school, the obligatory aptitude tests were not taken seriously—at least by me. I was thinking of marriage. When the guidance counselor sat down with the juniors and summarized individual aptitudes, he told me among other things that I could be a surgeon. It was as though he had suggested being an astronaut or submarine officer. It was outside the possibility of anything I could imagine. Much later, when career centers became full-blown operations and these sorts of interest-aptitude tests were available anytime, I learned that I could indeed have chosen many paths. My most surprising discovery as an academic dean, when on a whim I tried a computer version of "What should I do with my life?" was that I could have been a labor union organizer. Any college administrator would recognize the irony of that revelation.

Had I known in high school what I realized only much later—that my father would have liked to have studied to be a medical doctor—I might have been swayed toward science. Besides that was a more practical degree. But, without a career path in mind, I decided on literature with little rationale or logic by which I could defend the choice. Del knew me better than I knew myself, and he urged me to follow my inner nudges.

✛

California

It is always tempting, in reviewing the crossroads or forks in the path which lead to life choices, to create significance in insignificant things. Maybe that is the true meaning of Providence. I can only say that I was lucky in the parents I had who were adventurers and explorers in their own way; who dared to consider new paths and to ask questions without permission.

In 1952 when I was eleven, we moved from Oregon to California. My parents, along with a small group of likeminded members of the church, most of whom were related, were asked by the Pacific Coast Mennonite Mission Board to undertake a new venture—to begin a "rescue mission" in either San Francisco or Sacramento. Upon further consideration of these two sites, it was agreed that four families would move to California and establish a mission on Sacramento's Skid Row. The capitol city was notorious for a blighted area near the river which drew scores of folks suffering from failed hopes and miserable choices. Living in squalor, they were referred to as "down-and-outers." They included stupefied alcoholics, victims of a variety of derangements, and some from respectable families who had simply lost their way. The rescue missions that sprang up in Sacramento's inner city, forerunners to later homeless shelters and soup kitchens, became for these Oregon Mennonites an opportunity for service and preaching the gospel.

There was a great sense of adventure in my parents' move, along with some risk involved in renting out the farm and hoping for enough income to provide financial support. The church would have used the language of faith in this enterprise—and it was a journey of faith, without a doubt. But the western spirit of entrepreneurship was also an element which propelled these rural folks into the city. The old *insider/outsider* sensibilities were turned upside down. Suddenly we were the outsiders in the California culture.

The women undertook new roles as they partnered with their husbands in the work. They prepared sandwiches and coffee for the unshaven bums who showed up for nightly services at 1021 Second Street. They collected clothing for those in need. And they befriended the occasional woman who found her way to the Rock of Ages Rescue Mission. Plunged into a totally new environment, we children were allowed to help out in the kitchen before and after services, enduring long sermons to rub shoulders with the endlessly fascinating characters we came to know.

There was Little John who was a regular at the mission, with matted curly hair and a reserved disposition. He had a furtive manner which gave the impression that he walked sideways, looking out of the corner of his eye as though he could not bear to gaze directly at anyone. There was Elsie, a mound of a person, whose enormous body heaved itself onto the front bench in view of the kitchen. It was not clear which was more shocking to the children—her size or the fact that she talked freely about her chronic constipation. There were John and Mary, a devoted couple of limited mental abilities, who found a community among the mission families and became Mennonite converts. These were the people Christ would have served; there could be no doubt about it.

My home congregation back in the Willamette Valley did not exactly leap to support these mission families, the young visionaries, but neither did the Harrisburg church excommunicate us. With the assistance of the Pacific Coast mission board, this venture lasted six years, after which the families returned to farming and other occupations back in Oregon. The break with the Harrisburg church was essentially complete. My parents, back at their farm on Powerline Road, resumed extended family and community relationships but did not return to the Amish Mennonite congregation they had left. It was a time of new possibility.

The four families who had felt the call to begin a Skid Row mission also started a small Mennonite church in the Sacramento suburbs, inviting in the community. Other Mennonite families moved in to help with the work of this fledgling church community. They partnered in establishing a one-room elementary school for their children, housed in a garage on one of their properties. They built a half-way house for alcoholic converts from the mission who wanted "to go straight," as we would have said, and staffed the home with good decent people who dedicated themselves to serving the down-and-out. Our families worked with a local Black Baptist church in a community summer Bible school, which provided us children our first exposure to African-Americans. That in itself was not as memorable for me as observing baptism at the church, the Macedonia Baptist Church, a few miles from our home.

We joined the crowd one night, a sultry California night, for a baptism. It was a boisterous service leading up to the immersion ceremony. To Mennonites who practiced the sprinkling or pouring form of this rite, the Macedonia baptism was magnificent and spectacular. The elders had uncovered under the platform at the front of the church what seemed to me then a huge tank filled with water. The minister waded in. Each of the girls awaiting baptism, dressed in angel white, entered the pool in turn. It was an amazing sight. Without warning and with sleight-of-hand movements, the preacher took hold and pushed the body under, while at the same time giving a boost to the thrashing white figure struggling to surface. How did they know when to hold their breath, I wondered? We children could not take our eyes from the dripping bodies and the clinging white robes as each emerged to be embraced by their sisters and brothers.

✛

Growing Up and Liking it

The California years were my teen years. Community and church identity were never negotiable, but the change of scenery represented only the surface of how drastic was the move from the Willamette Valley to central California. In the unrelenting heat, a contrast to the mildness of the Oregon seasons, life flourished in the cherry and apricot orchard on the two-acre plot in the Rio Linda suburb where we lived. Up and down our street, neighbors welcomed us.

It was an errand to the Browns one afternoon that for me shifted the way the sun came up in the morning and the way it set in the evening. That particular day was hot. The patch of lawn in front of our redwood-sided ranch house belied the dryness of the season. My mother insisted on keeping the yard watered. The red, paint-chipped tubing of the sprinkler faithfully spun round hour after hour, with one of us assigned to pull it from one patch of green to another, according to the time allotted for each section. The clover responded quickly, springing up profusely. The fragrant white blossoms drew the honeybees. Barefoot in the summer, my sisters and I learned, after a few stings, to watch where we stepped whenever we headed out to the orchard.

This was the season of ripeness. The warm apricots hung from the trees along the drive. Mom and Dad picked the fruit, raked the drops which attracted the wasps, and tried to keep up with the customers who came to buy apricots and cherries. In our attached garage, jars of canned fruit lined the pantry shelves. The boiling canner in the tiny kitchen steamed the whole house to such an extent that, as often as my sisters and I could, we sought relief from the heat inside by escaping to the orchard shade or to the creek which ran along the back of our place.

Why I connect summer time with my errand to the Browns, I am not certain. Logically it does not exactly add up, because my birthday was not yet for several months. I had been helping with the canning, packing the raw apricots into Mason jars. We added the sugar syrup to each jar, with Mom doing the final step—wiping the rim and checking for nicks before putting on the lids. Satisfied, she twisted the screw bands firmly and placed each jar into near boiling water for the last canner of the day. It was four o'clock and there had been no escaping to the creek. Mom wiped the perspiration from her forehead with the back of her hand and set the timer on the stove. I calculated that I had an hour before she would be needing help with supper.

I had already collected the apricot pits, stems, and the odd scraps from the sink and then headed out to the compost pile in the orchard. This was my time to escape. But not for long. From the back porch, Mom called me back.

I picked up the old dented aluminum basin, swiped out the last of the peelings with my hand, and picked my way over the dirt clods in the orchard back to the path to the house. The sun was lower now, the direct rays broken by the neighbor's house providing some relief from the heat. "I want you to take this head of cabbage over to Mrs. Brown," my mother said. "She said she could use some. Don't stay long, now. I need you to help with supper pretty soon."

This was a welcome chore, for the Browns were favorite neighbors. Formerly they had lived in our very house. Then they divided the orchard, built themselves a new bungalow, and sold off a parcel. The Brown's house was cool and modern. It seemed stylish and elegant to a twelve-year-old used to simple furnishings showing the wear and tear of three girls and a little brother. I picked up my sandals as I headed for the shortcut through the cherry trees. Brushing back my hair, I rang the doorbell with one hand, balancing a huge cabbage in the other. I waited.

I knew that the Browns approved of the hardworking family who had taken over their orchard. Even we children, who squabbled constantly, felt friendly approval. The door opened and Dimple Brown brightened in welcome. "Come in." I had never before known a grown woman by the name Dimple. I had never known anyone, in fact, by that name. I handed Mrs. Brown the cabbage as she invited me in. I stepped into the cool kitchen, neat, without the clutter and steaminess of the endless canning at home. The patterned tiles of the kitchen floor were beautiful in contrast to our dull linoleum. Again smoothing back my hair, conscious of the damp strands which had escaped my braids, I turned to go. "Just a minute," Mrs. Brown said. "I want to send your mother that recipe I was telling her about."

At that moment, Mr. Brown walked into the kitchen to see who was there. Tall, lanky, his face weathered by the California sun and his years in the orchard, he was reserved compared to his talkative wife. I thought him attractive in some strange and mysterious way. "I haven't seen you for a long time," he said. "You are growing up. How old are you by now?"

"I will be thirteen," I replied, suddenly aware that this adult was talking to me as a person, not as just one of the neighbor children next door.

"Thirteen. Why you are going to be a teenager," he observed. "That means that you are a young lady."

By that time, Mrs. Brown had located the recipe and it was time to go. "Thank your mother for the cabbage." I took the recipe, said good-bye and closed the kitchen door behind me. A teenager. A young lady. I loved Mr. Brown that day for showing me a self I had not yet recognized.

Expressing the Inexpressible

Out of the ordinary stuff of everyday life arise encounters which turn one's world a degree or two. There is no apparent reason why these moments assume a life of their own. They crystallize as premonitions of a self yet unknown. They are visions, as a character in a favorite novel says, "that come to us only in memory, in retrospect."

There was such an experience in high school. I was seventeen. It was a clear day. I had just come out of the main classroom building. Whether I was coming from biology or Spanish is not a detail I now recall, but I can still feel the almost aching beauty of the moment. Was it the splendor of the evergreens that surrounded the campus? Or hormones? Could it have been an unexpected comment earlier that day by my favorite teacher?

The young English instructor was a recent addition to the faculty, along with her brilliant, blond husband, who was hired to teach math. The girls fell in love with both of them. These newcomers, just out of college, took a personal interest in their students and apparently felt there was no rule against becoming friends. We learned a lot from them. When Mr. Herr signed my yearbook, using the word *effervescent*, I had to look it up. I was not certain his description of me was a compliment.

Mrs. Herr was passionate about literature. She also had an impeccable sense of fashion that set her apart from all the other teachers. After class, she remarked on a new shirt waist I was wearing—a cotton print with a button-down collar. This was a dress cut from a McCall's pattern and sewed on my mother's

Singer, so the compliment was enough to make a farm girl slightly giddy.

There on the porch of the classroom building, about to head across the yard to the girls' dormitory, I was suddenly overcome by the sense that a great adventure lay ahead. The sky was bluer than I had ever seen it. There was a kind of soaring physicality to the moment—of suspense and of timelessness. Then the day settled down again and I put it out of my mind. There were no words at the time by which to examine the experience. It was simply, as a line from a hymn text says, "a pulse of being stirred."

I have come to believe in fortuities—a term for what someone has described as those "signs that call you: come further out, come higher up." Through circumstance, sheer good fortune, providence, accident, timing, even a misstep here and there, fortuities push us on. If we are lucky, they prod awareness; they open new vistas. The math teachers' dinner, the cabbage errand to the Browns,' and a seventeen-year-old's vision on the front porch of the high school administration building were such signs.

There was also the day I entered an American poetry class at the University of Oregon. Professor Griffith introduced what he described as the genius of American poetry. It was 1983. I was a forty-two-year-old academic on sabbatical, back in the classroom. I was studying for comprehensive exams. That day I found my seat a few rows from the back of the class. The lecture was pure Griffith. He scratched out a cryptic outline on the blackboard as introduction to the course on major poets Edward Taylor, Ralph Waldo Emerson, Henry Wadsworth Longfellow, Edgar Allen Poe, Edwin Arlington Robinson, Emily Dickinson, and Robert Frost.

Of all my graduate school professors, the most intimidating was Dr. Griffith. He had seen much of life and found most of it wanting. I still see the yellowed whites of his eyes and scraggly hair, his bowed shoulders, his worn and sagging jacket, as he shuffled down the hallway between office and classroom. In contradiction to first impressions, he spoke with booming self-confidence. Fear blended with near worship among his students, who bowed before his wisdom and vast knowledge. To this day, I do not claim to understand the power he possessed which could wilt students in his presence.

"The function of poetry is to de-familiarize the familiar and to express the inexpressible." To express the inexpressible: that day in class those words shimmered in the light; they hung suspended in the silence, conveying something of life itself. Griffith laid down his chalk and turned back to the class. It was an instant of distilled reality. Professor Griffith's words would forever represent an indescribable and irrepressible sense that understanding one's place was bound up with some currency of exchange which would account for the transcendent in the ordinary—which would reveal the mysteries of time and place.

✛

Africa—Time Out

In many ways life in an out-of-the-way village on the Equator was a combination of near boredom, mild deprivation, and the endless effort required in doing even the simplest things. It was what in U.S. government terms would be classified as a hardship assignment: no running water, only a few hours of electricity a day, malaria a constant threat, oppressive heat. Even so, arriving in July 1965 in Etinan, Nigeria, assigned to the Presbyterian Qua Ibo Secondary School for a teaching assignment, there was a sense of adventure to the whole enterprise. This was a placement by one of our church agencies, the fulfillment of Del's and my dream that we might undertake a term of service abroad.

It was also in 1965 when the first American troops arrived in Vietnam. By November antiwar demonstrations were widespread. But by now we were settling in a bush village in Africa and mostly oblivious to what was happening back home. We had embarked on an experience which served in a certain way as a "time out."

Back in Portland in spring 1965, when Del had wrapped up a two-year stint of teaching high school math, people who inquired about our move thought we were crazy to take two preschoolers to the jungle. We glibly recited the facts we had been given. We assured family and friends that Nigeria, newly independent with rich oil resources, was one of the most promising and stable countries in the whole of Africa. We were young—twenty-four and twenty-five—with unbounded energy and a willingness to tackle almost anything.

We were also naïve, as we soon learned when we deplaned in Lagos. Immediately several Nigerians pressed around us in the airport, offering to help expedite clearance in one line or another while admiring our two daughters, three and four years old. They clearly knew what they were doing. We sailed through the international checkpoints, amazed at the smooth entry. Our documents got stamped, our medical forms were checked, and all was well. Soon we spotted our host waiting for us outside customs. We collected our luggage, again with the help of the locals, and made our way to the transport van, impressed by the efficiencies which had introduced us to the country.

Our mission host, an American, observed all this with great amusement. We climbed into the van and headed into the city. Only then did Claire explain to us that the impressive assistance at every turn—including short-circuiting the long lines—was expressly for the purpose of a *dash*. The over-eager helpers were expecting a bribe, the system by which things got done in this place. Whether we gave them a small tip for helping with the luggage, I no longer remember. I do know that we were too inexperienced to have understood what was going on. Apparently they were too decent to enlighten us, or maybe they were in shock that all they got was profuse thanks from this nice American family.

Settling into the two-room house provided by the school, we were ready for anything. Maybe not prepared, but ready. Collecting rainwater off the roof provided all the water we needed until the dry season. Then Victor, one of the compound workers, carried water up from the stream to fill the holding tank. Heating water on the wood stove for baths, adjusting to the mosquitoes, learning to take in stride the flying ants or the giant cockroaches, and getting used to the transparent geckoes which took over the house at night—all this paled in comparison to the sheer beauty of the place.

Footpaths and sandy roads invited exploration of the dense tropical forest. These paths were lined with white and green-veined caladiums, interspersed with the pink-centered variety. Poinsettias grew year round. The bougainvillea and hibiscus were commonplace, but the wild red and orange *gloriosa*, a variety of lily in the *Colchicaceae* family, was a real find in the undergrowth and all the more prized for its rarity in the region. We soon became accustomed to the almost overpowering fragrance of the frangipani blooming outside the bedroom. Where the palm forest yielded a little space, the lace-leafed flame trees stretched out in spectacular silhouette.

Our kitchen was a separate building, connected to the cement block house by a covered walkway. Next to the kitchen and the privy, a papaya tree kept company with a pineapple plant. We scratched out a garden in a plot off the yard, finding out by experience that the cultivated vegetables we craved were incredibly hard to grow. We coaxed along corn, tomatoes, melons, pumpkin, and green peppers, but much of the produce was pathetic. It was much easier to put a pineapple top in the ground and to create a productive patch. In the steaminess of the bush everything except our garden grew profusely—even the slender tree trunks we cut down for clothesline poles sprouted. And everything decayed quickly, including the tin cans we disposed of in the compost pit out back. And bodies.

During a funeral at the Etinan church for one of the local ministers, attendants had to keep spraying floral scent around the casket because burial had been postponed a little too long. When a lizard drowned in our water tank and tainted the supply, we wished it would have decayed a little faster. Trying to ignore the putrid odor, we simply boiled and filtered the water as usual, chalking this up to ordinary inconveniences like ants in the sugar or bug-infested beans.

The romance of listening to the drumming from the village late into the night, lying under a mosquito net canopy, gave way to everyday routines: walking or riding bicycle to the school compound in the oppressive heat, checking periodically for mail at the town post office, making rounds at night on the girls' compound—one of our duties. The reality was that there was no place to go and little social life, so we learned to occupy the evening hours with reading, playing games and an occasional shared meal with the Indian couple at the school who learned that we enjoyed curry and who, themselves, were eager for friendship and to try American food.

Sometimes we got together with other expatriates: the British doctor and his family, the Scottish Presbyterian couple across the compound, Peace Corps folks and missionaries assigned to other towns and villages. We developed friendships with Nigerian colleagues and were invited to the principal's house for dinner. We were looking forward to an authentic African meal but discovered that the hostess intended to honor us by serving a Western meal—in this case it was British style food including minted peas and canned pears for dessert.

There were African feasts, wedding celebrations, and the hospitality of villagers offering palm wine, *cola nut*, and warm fruit drinks—*squash* they called it. We grew to love the spicy groundnut stew, goat and fish stews made with palm oil, plantain, the native pumpkin *endice*, and yam. We learned to tolerate *foo foo*, the fermented, pounded cassava root which served as a Nigerian staple. The learning went both ways. Our children were a source of endless curiosity to the school girls, whose dormitories bordered our yard. They called out to our daughters in their beautiful British English and could not resist touching Lori and Judy's white skin and stroking their hair.

In that first year, we discovered many things. Perhaps we learned more about ourselves than about a different culture. We experienced contentment in simple things and the satisfactions of making do: grinding and mixing our own peanut butter from scratch, making brown sugar, substituting all kinds of things to try to make a decent pie when we had no apples or peaches or berries or cherries. We pretended, in cutting up firm slightly ripe papayas, that they could serve as a passable substitute for carrot sticks. Actually, they were quite awful.

We learned the value of friendship and the delights of hospitality, both given and received. We relied on letters from home to maintain connections even though mail was unpredictable. When Del's father died a few months after we arrived in West Africa, we received a sympathy card before we got the telegram informing us of his death.

We were greatly enriched by the wide variety of people we met, from educators to health care workers to the village women who carried enormous bundles of wood and pots of water on their heads. There were the yard boys who cut vast expanses of grass with a machete, the meat vendor who cycled up to our kitchen periodically with a slab of warm meat straight from the butcher. By the time the white, hump-backed cattle had been driven down from the arid north for local butchering, the meat was mostly muscle and sinew. Occasionally, however, we got so hungry for the taste of beef that I bought a piece—only edible pressure-cooked or ground.

In this time out from the pace and pressures of American life, we learned more about those fortuities which call us out and point ahead to that which is yet unknown. Del's math teaching job was set when we arrived. Other courses got added to his assignment, but that was to be expected, we were told. When I was asked to take over a soon-to-be vacant bursar position, I was surprised because I had had no accounting or office experience. That seemed not to matter. So I was installed behind a desk next to the principal's and learned on the job their system of accounting.

The urbane, charming principal, Mr. Ekong, a man educated in London and a consummate professional, taught me much about leadership, about management, about working within a school system, about faculty and student relations. While I would never have to use the practical knowledge I gained about corporal punishment—central in the Nigerian system for managing school boys—the accounting procedures I learned would stand me in good stead much later as a university administrator.

✛

Chaos

There were other lessons ahead, but not by choice. It became apparent that there was growing political instability in the country. Far from the government centers, we were able to ignore most of this, but eventually ominous reports began to reach us. The Ibo tribe was threatening to secede and form a new country. The political mix was complex. For a Westerner it was impossible to sort out the strands of tribal loyalties and offenses, the effect of post-colonial influences, economic forces, or Christian and Muslim factors. Travel was always an uncertain proposition on the narrow bush roads. But now checkpoints were added, manned by armed officers who, on a whim, could subject anyone to a search. Reports of rebel fighting began to filter in, but still these skirmishes were far away and life in Etinan proceeded relatively normally.

Not until the U.S. embassy directed dependents, women and children, to evacuate the region did the mission group of which we were a part begin to consider implications for them. It was decided that the girls and I would leave with a family headed for northern Nigeria where their older children were in boarding school. Del and I had twenty-four hours to get ready for the trip and to pack a few things into barrels for later shipping if Del would have to leave suddenly. Del and a mission colleague would accompany us as far as the eastern region border and then return to their respective duties.

There was a kind of high-pitched intensity about the whole thing, but little fear until at one road block we all got hauled into the police station. We were aware of the rumor that had been circulating that some of the rebels had confused the term *missionary* with *mercenary*, thereby endangering the well-being of missionaries in going about their business. At the least, we understood that we were at the mercy of any authority or would-be-authority that had something to prove.

After hours of waiting at the police station, without explanation we were released, but the delay meant that we would not make it to the river in time that day for the border crossing into the next region. Reports of long lines to get across the bridge added to our anxiety, but we had no choice. We found an overnight guesthouse and prepared to rise early to get in the queue for the next day's crossing.

Farewell at the border meant not simply a separation from Del but also severing communication, not knowing if he were safe, and uncertainty about when we might be reunited. The trip north with the Amstutzes took five days in the Peugot station wagon, with three adults and four children. At each checkpoint, as we presented our documents, we said a prayer and held our breath. Somehow we found a satisfactory way to explain, when I handed over our family passport, why there were only three of us traveling instead of four.

This passport arrangement later proved problematic for Del. Back in the eastern region, he was essentially in the country without papers, having sent the passport with me. A knowledgeable and resourceful U.S. official understood the seriousness of Del's situation—being in a war zone without a passport. The embassy arranged temporary papers with strict instructions that as soon as we could we must redo our documents so that Del would have his own passport.

After good-byes at the river crossing, Del returned to his teaching duties at the Qua Ibo Secondary School. Up north, kindly folks associated with the Jos international school, where our mission children attended, took us in. We settled into waiting and making a temporary life. Surely the war could not last longer than a few weeks, we thought.

We were not prepared for what followed. Biafra seceded.

Bridges were destroyed, harbors blockaded, and food withheld from the rebel population. The starving children of Biafra became familiar and heart-wrenching cover stories worldwide, emblems of the insanity and horror of war. Still the rebels held out, willing to die for their cause.

Del stayed in Etinan until the schools closed but left before the soldiers arrived to ransack the compound. He made his way out with a British tea merchant, crossing the river by canoe since the Onitsha Bridge where we had said good-bye was no longer passable.

Back in Jos, my daughters and I waited, with an occasional communiqué from Del—one to tell me that our close Michigan friends, Apostolic Lutherans who lived a few miles from Etinan, had been in a car accident on the way back from Lagos. Phil Johnson was dead. His wife and two young children had come back to the mission house to prepare for a return to the States. Del was helping them pack up. He also tried to distract the Johnson children by playing games with them, while Naomi interrupted the packing to receive the wailing women who came to mourn and to pay their respects. Much of this I learned only later, since the initial news of the accident had come to me in Jos via a radio transmission that Del had arranged through the Lutheran mission.

Up north, my daughters and I continued to wait and to hope. Too young to understand the larger scene, they prayed each night that their dad would be kept safe and come soon. The days, then weeks, of waiting stretched out. One evening after supper, about six weeks after we had arrived in Jos, a big Chevrolet taxi pulled up to the front door. Del climbed out with a couple suitcases. His return was all that mattered at that moment. It was only in bits and pieces that we heard the story of how he had gotten out of Etinan to make his circuitous way down to Lagos, the capitol city, where he could catch a flight north.

✙

Home

It was 1968, a year to be described four decades later as the "pivotal turning point of an era," a time of turbulence and tragedy. One April morning I switched on the radio, tuning in to the Voice of America. This was our best connection to updates from the U.S. We were in Jos, finishing up our interrupted three-year term by teaching at the Baptist High School. The war was still grinding on in other areas of Nigeria. The news brief I had expected was not being broadcast, nor was there an explanation of the deviation from the usual programming. Only music of a formal military-like dirge came over the air waves. It was ominous. Something surely had gone wrong. A global catastrophe? A world war?

It was very like the terrible feeling I would experience as an eight-year-old coming home from school only to discover everyone gone. As children we had absorbed dire predictions of the end times from our church's belief in biblical prophecy. In the two minutes it took me to comb the house and, with growing desperation, call out for my mom, I would become panic stricken. I feared that the Matthew 24 prophecy had come to pass, the one that warned that when two shall be out working together, one will be taken and the other left behind. The "rapture," the return of the Lord, was the theme of many a revival sermon describing the consequences of resisting salvation. These sermons fed our deepest fears and insecurities.

That day in the kitchen, bent over the short wave radio, some of those dark terrors were stirred. Then we heard the news. Martin Luther King Jr., had been assassinated. That report from home, horrifying and unfathomable, framed the plans and expectations that were forming for our return to the U.S. in June. While completing our teaching and office assignments, we found ourselves yearning for home, longing to see family and friends. It had been a hard year, and it was time.

Now our daughters were in grade one and in kindergarten. They had few memories of the Oregon valley or of their grandparents. We had planned for months to return to the U.S. by way of Europe, allowing ourselves a little vacation in Switzerland and London. It was in Thun, a castle town, that we first saw the newspaper photos of Robert Kennedy being shot. The Swiss proprietor of our little hotel, in answer to our question, "Was Robert Kennedy killed?" told us that she thought that he had not died. Language was limited on both sides, so it was not until we arrived in Zurich where we were able to find English speakers that we got the details and the confirmation that Robert Kennedy, too, had been assassinated.

By the time we got to London a week later, we discovered on a visit to Madame Tussaud's Museum that the wax artists had managed to create a temporary exhibit with full-bodied likenesses of Martin Luther King Jr. and Robert Kennedy. We were returning home with mixed feelings—reminded that the violence we were leaving behind in Nigeria was simply a different version of what awaited at home. For us the world had gotten both smaller and bigger. That fall the Apollo 7 spacecraft had made history as its three astronauts were launched into orbit. The moon walk the following summer, which we all watched with incredulity, had something of the same impact.

We were reminded of our tiny presence in the grand scheme but were inspired by the magnificence of an effort which could put a man on the moon. The courage of the astronauts, the precision of science, and the wonder of that suspended blue world for the first time glimpsed from outer space ensured that we would never see things quite the same again.

Both the Biafran War and the Vietnam War slogged on interminably, it seemed. Three years out of the country meant a lot of catching up. The times were threaded with irony—the 1967 Summer of Love in San Francisco juxtaposed with the slaughter in Southeast Asia; the New Age movement blossoming in a marijuana haze against a backdrop of violence. The same month that Martin Luther King Jr. was assassinated, the Bureau of Narcotics and Dangerous Drugs was formed to curb the surge in illegal drug use. Earlier that year, 5,000 women had marched on Washington to demand an end to the Vietnam War.

Sometime after our return to the U.S., Del and I took a weekend excursion to San Francisco with high school friends. There in Haight-Ashbury, center of the hippie movement, we saw for ourselves things as strange as anything we had observed in West Africa. Attending a performance of the first rock musical, *Hair,* we sensed, if not fully understood, the convergence of forces in American society which gave expression to a desperate hope, overshadowed by anger and despair. Subtitled *The American Tribal Love-Rock Musical, Hair* tapped into a growing realization that the morass in Vietnam was sucking the life out of the American soul and spirit. "I believe in love," the performers sang, then: "Hey, hey, LBJ, how many kids did you kill today?" It may have been the dawning of the "Age of Aquarius," evoking harmony and understanding, sympathy and trust, but for some it felt more like the end of the world.

PART THREE

THE LARGE QUESTIONS

Fate, Destiny, and Calling

"Is life's purpose something you create or discover?" a professor used to ask her students. Another version of the question might be, "Do we discover or create our destiny?" Growing up in a farm family with faith a central focus, that question would not have crossed my mind. Life simply unfolded the way it was supposed to. It was definitely a more "take what comes" approach than any sense that we were players in our own evolving journey. It was to some extent an inexcusably lazy view, bolstered by the Scriptures which I seized for reassurance: "And we know that all things work together for good, to those who love God." This was a favorite during my teen years when I was just discovering that I was normal after all.

Shadowing my childhood was the perception that something was wrong with me. I was unusually small for my age. *Puny* would be the word the aunts would have used. My size was commented on, endlessly it seemed, by acquaintances of my parents or by relatives who were well-meaning, if insensitive: "If you don't hurry up and grow, your sister will catch up to you." The truth was my sister, two years younger, was already almost my height. I developed a deep and abiding longing just to be normal—to be like everybody else. It was not until well into high school that I began to understand that size does not determine all and that being small can be turned to advantage.

I see now that the Mennonite community served as a kind of cocoon, providing the protection and isolation by which one could put aside most of the questions of "why?" and "how?" We learned early that Scripture always provided appropriate answers, and we did not question our destiny as children of God. Yet there were threads of uneasiness as I moved toward adulthood and observed the dire callings and undeviating commitments of those who, without a trace of humility, felt singularly called and empowered by God. It seemed more than presumptuous to assume that God orders a clear path—downright dangerous, in fact, as the line between dedication and derangement was sometimes murky. At least it appeared so to me. The illusion of destiny is not a matter I take lightly. On the other hand, I have never been able to dismiss the inscrutability and the surprise of my experience suggesting that life is more than a chain of accidents.

My initiation into the mystery of providence was not marked by a single incident or by a series of coincidences. Rather, the seeds of mystery were sown in a mounting awareness that pointed to something beyond, to something more. I had made my peace with the Scriptures which conveyed God's plan for humankind. I had taken comfort, even as a child, that someday the unknown would be known and God would be fully revealed. Although I was put off by what seemed to be the apostle Paul's boasting of his special call, I could not discount Paul's Damascus Road transformation.

But it was the Old Testament narratives of heroes who were selected to tackle unimaginably difficult tasks that drew me in—Esther taking her life in her hands to confront King Ahasuerus, Jael fortuitously positioned to kill an enemy who had taken shelter in her house. (Driving a spike through the army commander's head while he slept has always seemed to me one of the more glamorously gruesome accounts in Scripture.) In these narratives, waters parted and armies were conquered, the dead were restored to life, giants were slaughtered, and the God of the Hebrews demonstrated on a vast canvas of blood and gore that the Almighty called out individuals for special tasks.

These stories were real to me, not simply because they were the stuff of years of Sunday school and summer Bible school but also because the characters in these dramas suffered, they questioned, they anguished, they argued with God. The call of God was sometimes ambiguous, needing testing. At times hand-picked individuals were asked to do the unthinkable to partici-pate in God's grand scheme. Sometimes one of these characters refused to do what God asked. All this seemed more real, some-how, than the clear-eyed view of the preachers who always seemed so sure. And in their sureness, they disagreed with oth-ers who were equally sure.

I shall always love my father-in-law for a question he dared ask out loud. His religious commitments were of a decidedly conservative bent. He demonstrated unswerving loyalty to the Mennonite church with its set of rules and regulations. He was strict. He was also stubborn, his son would say. One day in a conversation about some finer point of church doctrine and his own beliefs, he asked, "What if I am wrong?" Suddenly the world seemed a finer and more compassionate place. I never viewed my father-in-law in quite the same way after that.

The tussle with Scripture on the way to adulthood con-firmed my beliefs and, paradoxically, at the same time fed the questions which lay submerged for the most part beneath the demands of family, job and church. I was amid one of those episodes where life gets muddier and clearer at the same time. It was 1995. I was sitting in the Eastern Mennonite University auditorium. There in the chapel service, the congregation duti-fully located the reading printed in the back of the hymnal. It was No. 823, an excerpt from Psalm 139. Certainly not an un-familiar text. But that day, the words jolted me in their timeli-ness. Surely this was not mere coincidence? These were the weeks leading up to my interview for the Bluffton presidency. I was ambivalent about the urging of the Bluffton search com-mittee to become a candidate for the position. A college presi-dency was not on my list of next things to consider as Del and I came to a decision to make a change.

"O Lord, you have searched me and you know me," read the congregation. "You discern my going out and my lying down. . . . Before a word is on my tongue you know it completely, O Lord. You hem me in—behind and before; you have laid your hand upon me. . . . Where can I go from your Spirit? Where can I flee from your presence?" I sat there overcome by the sense that things were not in my control and, even more startling, that the Creator in infinite wisdom had written in the book of time and timelessness "all the days ordained for me . . . before one of them came to be."

Certain phrases from the Psalm became my mantra over the next days as I tried to prepare for the upcoming interview, as I attempted to anticipate the search committee's questions and worried about how I would do on the spot. After all, it was not an eagerness for the position that was driving me; it was rather the conviction that one does not lightly say no to the church. I knew that I had to go through with the interview at least—learning about this Midwest Mennonite college directly and giving them a chance to examine me.

One of my besetting sins is the need to be prepared, to not let things up to chance if I can help it. How does one prepare? The best I could do was to settle down with the materials Bluffton had sent to acquaint myself with the organization and begin outlining my questions. In preparation for the interview, I would have opportunity by telephone to raise any specific issues in advance with the board chairman and search committee chair. Those included questions such as "What are the trustees' most important agenda items in seeking a new president? What are those of the faculty? Are they the same?" I needed to determine, as a female candidate, if there were gender issues to consider. Was the constituency open to a woman president, breaking a nearly 100-year tradition of male leaders? What would be the expectations for a president who does not have a "wife"? What would be the most pressing matters for attention in the two years before re-accreditation?

It was a dreary September Saturday when I flew from Washington, D.C., to Cincinnati for the interview. All the way there, I kept returning to lines from Psalm 139 as assurance that the Creator already knew how it was going to turn out and that whatever words I would need in the exchange were already registered with God. I found this immensely comforting. At one point I found myself wondering what God knew that I would say, having drawn confidence from a literal rendering of Psalm 139: "Before a word is on my tongue you know it completely, O Lord." I was ready to see what might happen.

I was met at the Cincinnati airport by the chairman of the board of trustees who was hosting the search committee in his law offices located in the center of the city. This part of the story is curious in itself. The chair of the board was an old acquaintance from the one year he spent in graduate school at the University of Oregon, 1969-70, studying math. It was in math class that he had met Del. Now more than twenty-five years later, with very little association in between, we were to meet again.

I had tried to memorize the names and positions of the interviewers which included church representatives, college trustees, educators, attorneys, entrepreneurs, and faculty representatives. It was, at first glance, a large and formidable committee. Their job was to find a successor to a longstanding president who was retiring after thirty successful years at the institution—as a faculty member, as an academic dean, and then as president.

Toward the end of the day as conversations were moving toward conclusion, I knew that my forthright responses to some of their questions had given them a sense of who I was. Had I been too candid? Had I been too quick to say, "I don't know"? I knew less about them, clearly, than they about me. My friend Ed, the board chair, ushered me up to a private conference room on the fourteenth floor of the Taft, Stettinius, and Hollister suite. It was 4:30 p.m. by now. I remember waiting there alone, rain pelting the plate glass windows. It was nearly dark outside. Finally, after what seemed a long time of deliberation by the search committee, the board chair and the search committee chair returned to report that, if I agreed, they would like to continue the conversation and move to the next step of the process.

Though I cannot be certain, I surely must have collected my wits enough to express appreciation for the congenial committee and the depth of the discussion throughout the day. I remember only two simple, very private questions. It came down to this, I told them: "Can I do the job?" And, "Do I want to do it?"

The clarity which came to me in that final exchange as the search committee left to go their separate ways—to Indiana, Kansas, Pennsylvania, and Ohio—was freeing in a strange way, preparation for the next stages of the process when I would meet with board members, with faculty and staff, and with students. I know from hindsight the importance of honoring the questions; that one steps aside to make room for uncertainty and those pressing probes which reflect unease, confusion, anxiety, and sometimes sheer terror.

Three Questions

"Love the questions," Rilke said. I have learned to live the questions and to love them, too. I realized one day that three unexpected questions trace the trajectory of my experience. Can a life be summed up so simply? Or is it more accurate to say that these three questions capture the decision points that belie any temptation to think of my life as just unfolding willy nilly?

The first one was my father's when he questioned the wisdom of going to school when my marriage plans were in place. "Why do you want to go to college?" It was not a "Let's think through this, carefully; are you sure this is practical?" It was rather a challenge to what appeared to be a lack of common sense. And common sense in our family was highly prized. My determination to get at least one year of college before getting married to my high school sweetheart was a departure from tradition. I was signaling that what my mother had achieved and the role she had played in being the consummate housewife and dutiful, generous mother were not enough.

If my dad had pressed me on what I would study, I would have been at a loss. I eventually selected classes in home economics (a respectable course of study for women in that time), in Bible, in music, and in marriage and family. Biology and English rounded out my courses. That first year of college, however, was really about leaving home and about being sure that the door would remain ajar for further education. It was also a year for my fiancée and me, engaged at ages nineteen and eighteen, to spend time together.

"Why do you want to go to college?" was the question that summoned an awareness that I needed to make my own decisions, even though those decisions were not logical, clearly thought out, or even fully understood at the time.

The second distilling question was my mother's, "Will you have a good man to work for?" I love this question because it is as much about my mother as it is about me. Twelve years before I would be weighing the invitation to a college presidency, I had been asked to take on the academic dean role at Eastern Mennonite College. Up until then, my mother knew that I kept going to school and that I worked in an office and sometimes taught a class. That all fit within her framework of service in a church-related school. Though unacquainted with appointments and responsibilities in the higher education arena, she instinctively knew that an academic dean was a man and that my taking such a position was departing from the prescribed roles that assured the scriptural order for men and women.

My mother's query continues as an important reminder that I owe much to two world views: that of a faith community committed to hierarchical roles and also to a belief that individuals are called out for God's purposes—sometimes against the grain of embedded religious and cultural strictures. The tension could be wrenching, but it was life-giving also as I matured in my understanding of what God might be asking me to do.

The third question, already introduced, represents another one of those decision points, the importance of which is only understood in retrospect. "Why would you want to do this?" The question amused me; it also startled me. I tried to dismiss it as the curious, make-conversation query of a woman who had sized me up when she learned I was at Bluffton for campus interviews. Now, after much secrecy as these searches go, I had been identified as the presidential candidate. Del and I sat there in the Marbeck student center with the trustee wife, waiting to be summoned to the Board reception—our first meeting with the trustees. Whatever small talk we made as we sat there has been long forgotten. But not the woman's question: "Why would you want to do this?" The question was direct, polite and conveyed a hint of sympathy. Yes, "why?"—with the implication being, "Why would you, a woman, want to take on the messiness of running a school?"

This provocative introduction to the interviews to follow remained in the back of my mind the entire weekend. It was also a question that I periodically found myself hauling out over the years for further scrutiny. It was a worthy question. And one which I got better at answering.

Heading into the reception, Del and I were introduced and welcomed warmly. I tried to keep sorted out in my mind the names and occupations of the trustees: the landscape architect who designed zoos, the manufacturer of buses, the three attorneys, the high school principle, the furniture salesman, the pastor, the corn farmer, the retirement home administrator, the university history professor, the Marathon Oil economist, the tomato producer, a couple wealthy businessmen and representative church leaders.

It would take me years in the presidency before I would be able to fully comprehend and appreciate the answer to the trustee wife's question. I have thanked Marie, who became a dear friend, for her bold curiosity that day. The answer to her "why?" is based, really, on a growing sense of gratitude for an opportunity to serve a noble enterprise and to be a part of a larger life beyond oneself.

But again I am getting ahead of the story.

+

Nudges

We were back in graduate school, Del and I, having returned to Eugene ten years after moving to the East Coast. In the early 1970s, Del and I and our two daughters left Oregon and headed to Virginia for my husband's first college appointment. As western transplants, we understood that we were somehow different but did not spend much time figuring out how. I missed the Oregon rain and the green fields, but the unspoiled beauty of the Shenandoah Valley contributed to an easy transition. Our family settled in and Virginia was becoming home.

Conveniently, I got a job as assistant to the dean at Eastern Mennonite along with teaching a few courses, once I had completed my Master's degree at James Madison University next door. I discovered that much of what I had learned from my super-organized mom applied to administration—be clear about the task, follow through, and get the job done. This position, which I got almost by accident when a vacancy suddenly came open, proved to be a curious mix of tedious detail and exhausting (though often inspiring) interpersonal relationships. The endless variety of tasks and the constant challenge of tackling something new was a happy mix.

Occasionally a sense of restlessness would sneak up on me, although I was mostly successful in ignoring it. I was having a great deal of fun. But the nudge to consider a change, after a number of years, grew stronger. Besides, Oregon continued to have a pull. Now 1982, it was time for Del's first sabbatical, so the two of us arranged combined sabbaticals supplemented by a leave of absence. This gave us two years to return to the University of Oregon. We would become students again in a town of aging hippies and counterculture hangers-on. At the edge of the Willamette Valley, pressing almost into the forests at the lower reaches of the Cascades, we would live in a tiny apartment and simplify our lives—no committee meetings, no community or church obligations. Del, being urged by the dean to prepare to teach business in addition to math, would work toward an MBA; and I would return to study what I loved.

I was granted a teaching fellowship in the English department to pursue a Ph.D. in literature. That decision in itself had been difficult. Much earlier, the choice of study had been between science and English. Now I had to choose again. Back at Eastern Mennonite, colleagues in my job offered conflicting advice. "Go back in higher education," one of the vice presidents advised me. Another said, "I don't know why you would need a doctorate," this from one of the top women academics in the institution. If I were going to invest the time to get the Ph.D., then a practical choice made sense, I thought—a degree in higher education. But I kept arguing with myself. I began to doubt that I could endure the prospect of all the professional education requirements if I chose the administrative degree. This internal debate was being carried on both consciously and subconsciously as I continued to test the options with trusted confidants.

Finally one day the dean, who had been encouraging all the way, put it clearly: "Go with what you really want to do." This was permission. This was confirmation. Knowing I had no plans for a career in English, this was another turning point in which I abandoned logic and reason in favor of some inner sense that I really had no choice—the path was already being marked out.

✦

In a Dark Time

The small group of us that began Ph.D. studies that fall of 1982 were aghast to hear almost immediately the reports of how dismally the previous year's entering class had done on their "qualifiers," comprehensive examinations required of entering doctoral students at the end of their first year. A web of rumors alerted us that the department was cracking down, redesigning the exams and upping the requirements.

For me the course of action was clear. It meant not only the necessity of a refresher of all the English courses I had ever taken, but of making up for deficiencies in undergraduate studies when I had messed around with world literature, folklore, biblical literature, and other topics instead of plowing through English Survey I, II, and III and the basic sequence of American Literature courses. So, in addition to regular courses and carrying out my duties as a graduate teaching assistant, I set out to tackle an impossible reading list—some make-up, some review—of all the authors and works that I should know from medieval times to the present.

Some nights I fell asleep trying to keep straight the plots and subplots of Spenser's *Faerie Queene*. Other times, I was just grateful that George Elliot's *Middlemarch* or *Daniel Deronda* had a plot one could follow and—if one were lucky—could remember at least the names of the main characters. In class, Professor Weatherhead's passion for W. H. Auden, Christopher Isherwood, and Stephen Spender carried me along.

On other days, Dr. Griffith's grizzled presence in the Transcendental Seminar evoked dread and terror because not only did I know virtually nothing about the transcendentalists, but their abstractions and dialectics left me confused and dizzy. I was not ready for Emerson's dissertations on the Oversoul, on becoming a Universal Being, on the transparent eyeball. "What is the meaning of the loon's call?" Dr. Griffith would ask. He would fix his rheumy eyes on us and wait for erudite responses. One or two of the students in that class seemed to be able on cue to spew forth the most learned commentary on Heidegger or Hegel, making applications and connections to the text under discussion. The rest of us listened in paralyzed amazement, the walls in the crowded seminar room closing in.

✛

Dreams and Nightmares

Then began a recurring dream. Ascending a steep mountain, I would be making steady progress. Suddenly I would find myself falling off backward as I approached the summit. My freefall was interrupted only by waking sweaty and cold. A natural fear of heights exacerbated the power of these nightmares. Or maybe it was the other way around? Some days I felt as though I existed in two equally fearsome realms: the world of night terrors or, on waking, being submerged in what seemed impossible demands of the first-year program. For months, embarking on this course of study seemed more like a sentence than liberation to pursue what I loved.

Then I discovered Theodore Roethke, an American poet, who had put into words what I could dimly feel but not express. Certain lines served as an incantation to sanity; they became my rosary beads, my Lord's Prayer. "I wake to sleep and take my waking slow . . . I learn by going where I have to go" ("The Waking"). These words comforted me in some inexplicable way.

As a way to hang on, to keep my courage up, I returned again and again to Roethke, who in the poem "In a Dark Time" speaks of meeting his "shadow in the deepening shade," of knowing "the purity of pure despair . . . / The edge is what I have."

At times I feared I was going mad. I couldn't sleep. I couldn't eat. Some nights late I would crawl into bed and Del would hold me. "He must know," I would think. A persistent tingling in my arms and legs had sent me to a neurologist who eventually ruled out MS. He did not ask me if I was under undue pressure, nor did he propose a remedy for my symptoms.

"Am I losing my mind?" I would ask Del. "Of course not," he would answer, not daring to admit his own fears. "Let's walk." Then we would leave our second floor flat, head over the bridge spanning the bike path. We would leave behind the books, the reading lists, the class assignments and head out. We walked for blocks and blocks, for miles and miles, up into the rolling hills of west Eugene. We trekked through the Oregon mists in the fall, through more drizzle in the winter, and traced the southwest perimeter of the city.

One night, after a period when I could hardly bring myself to eat, Del insisted we take the whole evening off. Much as he had done when I was nauseously pregnant years before and he had had to force feed me on one occasion, now he carted me off to the Red Lion for dinner. A real dinner. The persistent, hard knot lodged in the center of my chest relaxed just a little; the warmth of the whisky in our Turkish coffees helped. Then we went to see a long, long movie.

We sat through *Gandhi,* which I only remember because that evening remains etched in my mind as a crossroads. Either I was going to make it or I was not, and I would have to let go of something. In whatever it was that drove such single-minded pursuit of a goal, I was meeting my shadow and confronting fear: fear of failure, fear that I would never again be my normal self, fear that I had forever lost my energy and sense of well-being. My body was suffering and as though it were somehow separate from me, I felt pity for the pathetically thin frame, now not able to maintain even a weight of ninety pounds.

Each morning, by sheer power of will, I gathered my books and class notes and headed for the library and my assigned study carrel. The discipline of attending class, turning in assignments, and following a rigid study schedule kept me going.

That and my best friend, my life partner. Del never allowed whatever he might have been thinking to feed my fears.

There were interludes of peace and some personal rewards in those months. I continued to do well in my courses, tried to keep up with the paper grading in my English composition classes, and kept at the review for the spring comprehensive exams. Del was enjoying his studies, and I envied him the ability to take it all rather casually. We usually studied the entire weekend, only occasionally traveling up to Albany or Salem or Harrisburg to visit family.

One Saturday, amid this dark time, I felt an overwhelming urge to go home. I called my mom and asked if we could come for dinner on Sunday. I was never brave enough to confess to her how much I needed just to be in familiar surroundings again, to sit at her Sunday dinner table. Del did not seem to need any explanation, which I could not have given him actually, but he simply knew better perhaps than I did myself that I had to go home—that I had to make some attempt to recover myself.

That spring, we continued walking, heading up Eighteenth Avenue, turning over on Cleveland past the faded frame houses, up into the Eugene heights where the homes were spacious and the lawns meticulous. The spring flowering worked its own miracle—Japanese cherry trees, white and rose camellias, yellow and red tulip beds, purple plum flowers, and the sculpted blaze of scarlet azaleas. I began to feel again. The nightmare of climbing that formidable mountain returned only occasionally; I always woke before I smashed to the ground. I was able to take some control of myself, becoming more patient with what I could and could not do. My request to give up teaching responsibilities the quarter I would be taking my exams was granted. I was learning, as Roethke said, that "A man goes far to find out what he is." I was discovering something about the tests we put ourselves through. I was beginning to understand that fragility and strength are two sides of the coin and that it was necessary to embrace both.

Excelling in graduate school was what I demanded of my-self. But I learned far more than an appreciation for Wallace Stevens and Williams Carlos Williams; for John Henry New-man or Charles Darwin and the Victorians—or for the venerable professors who in rare instances became friends, not just mentors and teachers. The interlude of those two years back at the university served in many ways as a retreat from "the real world." There were times I felt as though I were in monastic seclusion, subject to unspoken and desperate vows. Perhaps this was a necessary process of submitting to the Refiner's fire (a perfectly good term in our religious community) and of yielding to a course in soul-making? At the time, I could not have known that this was preparation for work that I could not yet imagine.

✛

Identity: the Education of a
Mennonite Farmer's Daughter

Returning to Oregon periodically for study at the university provided opportunity for time with extended family on both sides—our parents and brothers and sisters. I learned among other things, that one's sense of self is constantly evolving. One's identity is never fixed, and that is a good thing. Here I was, returning for graduate studies in my early forties, sitting in classrooms with twenty and thirty-something's. It was comforting, I admit, that my office mate who was also a graduate assistant and working on her doctorate was in her sixties. It provided me with the illusion, at least, of not being so old after all.

Well into my first year of Ph.D. studies, I knew that I would need to select a dissertation topic. I had been drawn to a contemporary California writer who, in addition to being a novelist, was one of the rising practitioners of what was being called the "new journalism"—an approach that incorporated the personal in contrast to the long-standing journalism standard of objective reporting. I was particularly attracted to Joan Didion because she explored the inner boundaries of the Western sensibility and the spirit which had driven settlers west in the first place.

I was lured by her ability to read the cultural, political, geographical, and psychological landscape of California, probing the awful sense of "manifest destiny" demonstrated by the pioneers who endured unimaginable hardships. The account of the Donner Party figured large in Didion's imagination in unraveling the history of California's development. Traveling from the

Midwest to California in 1846, the Donner Party had reached the Sierras, when they were forced by a sudden blizzard to halt their journey. Faced with starvation, they resorted to eating their own dead. The fragile and often needy characters that were characteristic of Didion's fiction and nonfiction helped me put in perspective my own short immersion in the California scene, when my parents were serving a conglomeration of strange and desperate souls in the Sacramento mission on Second Street.

"Why would anyone want to fill his mind with this?" asked one of my professors, baffled by my interest in Didion as I moved toward finalizing my research topic. Dr. Weatherhead found her view of life singularly depressing. At the formal defense of my dissertation, I was expected to provide a few introductory remarks about my subject. I took up Dr. Weatherhead's question, noting that the surreal quality of California life as Didion described it (and as I had observed it as a teenager) was one aspect that interested me. The themes of the West and what made westerners different were even more important in attracting me to her writing. But it was more. I told my examiners that in Didion I had discovered a mode of knowing which is personal—something academicians are not very good at talking about. Reading *Slouching Toward Bethlehem* or *The White Album*—chiseled essays about the '60s—I found they were reading me as well. I was discovering something more about who I was through the unlikely perceptions of a writer for whom faith was not any kind of answer.

Didion's essays demonstrated a bent toward the extraordinary and the apocalyptic, a sensibility not so far from the dire perspective of the revival preachers I had grown up with. In portraying characters driven by emptiness and a search for meaning, she captured the spiritual blight infecting society—again a familiar perspective of my secluded religious upbringing that emphasized the Fall. It was not so much the lostness of her characters that appealed to me as it was Didion's hard-eyed view of the human condition, her ability to stare evil in the face and not be destroyed; it was her refusal to be comforted by romantic illusions that seemed true to what I knew about the world around me. Against the backdrop of extremes, she gave attention to the ordinary and to the practical conditions of our lives, never preaching but dealing with moral concerns that could only be viewed as a search for the transcendent.

Finally, I was taken in by Joan Didion's ability to ask the large questions: What does it mean? Where are we headed? How did we get from there to here? I identified with her recognition of those "unspeakable mysteries" (her term) which are part of our experience. I concluded my introductory comments to the dissertation committee that day, in May 1985, by referring to John Gardner's statement in *On Moral Fiction* on why we read literature anyway: "True art clarifies life, establishes models of human action, casts nets toward the future, carefully judges our right and wrong directions, celebrates and mourns." That is still the best explanation I know of why I read novels and why I love literature.

My immersion in the dissertation project was as much a personal journey as it was an academic exercise. Because I was always catching up, having spread out my college and graduate studies on into midlife, perhaps I was doomed in some perverse way to take my education personally and to take myself too seriously.

The positive side of that, however, was that the interaction with professors and fellow students had a way of throwing me back to my roots as I continued to sort out who I was. As an undergraduate in the late '60s and early '70s, and then as a graduate student later in the '80s, I was shaped by remarkable mentors. I first learned to know Dr. Roland Bartel in undergraduate studies. This English professor discovered I was a Mennonite and took a special interest in my studies, he himself having attended Bethel College, a Mennonite institution. He also had served as a conscientious objector in CPS (Civilian Public Service) during World War II. Biblical literature was one of his interests as it was of Professor Stanley Maveety, who was so engaging in his knowledge of and respect for the Old Testament that I took three courses from him.

A literary approach to Scripture was not threatening but increased my awareness that the old Sunday school versions did great injustice to the depth and wonder of Holy Scripture. In contrast to the often one-dimensional, safe view of God that fit neatly with the tenets of my congregation, I saw for the first time the splendor of the Bible and the beauty of ambiguity.

This was illustrated one day in class by Professor Maveety introducing us to contrasting Old Testament texts regarding the inclusion or exclusion of foreigners. We examined the story of Ruth, a Moabite foreigner, who became a part of the Hebrew family and the foremother of Jesus himself. How do we reconcile the account of Ruth, the professor asked, with that of the book of Ezra in which foreign wives and their children were ruthlessly expelled to purify the Hebrew community in their sin of intermarriage? The simple juxtaposition of these two stories, with a scholarly comparison of time periods and the historical setting, was a seminal moment for me, revealing a God that was much larger than the constricted view with which I had grown up.

Returning to the classroom in my late twenties to finish my undergraduate studies proved fortuitous timing. The Africa experience contributed to an interest in other literatures and a better understanding of world cultures. Since my daughters were in elementary school and Del back in graduate school, I could immerse myself in study. In certain ways, I was still living out an unexamined faith—able to shuck off any troubling philosophies that did not fit into the Christian framework.

Existentialist philosophy and its inherent nihilism was the lens through which my Modern American Writers professor, Dr. Handy, taught Faulkner and Hemingway. I could appreciate the symbolic myth of Sisyphus condemned forever to moving a boulder up the mountain, only to have it dislodge at the top and roll back to the bottom. Illustrative of the human dilemma of eternal struggle—and to some it represented a meaningless struggle—the myth did not satisfy me, however, as an explanation of reality.

It was my religious beliefs that provided a balancing dimension. I simply adapted what I was learning in the classroom to my personal faith understandings. I did not find this paradoxical, or particularly difficult. It seemed possible to weigh and appreciate contradictory philosophies while at the same time remaining true to one's religious commitment. Perhaps a more crass way of looking at this would be F. Scott Fitzgerald's famous observation that "the test of a first-rate intelligence is the ability to hold two opposed ideas in the mind at the same time, and still retain the ability to function."

It was not unusual in those undergraduate days to find the biblical text incorporated into the curriculum on a number of levels, whether it was Jewish literature, drama, world surveys or Dr. Maveety's biblical literature sequence. I do not recall the particular course, but I do remember a classmate's thinly disguised irritation in a question he asked me one day after class was dismissed. We were studying the Book of Job and Job's trials. My friend was identifying with Job and his anguished cries directed at a God who would permit such personal devastation to one of the faithful. "How can you believe in such a God?" he asked. This student could not comprehend that the voice out of the whirlwind was any answer at all, nor that it was a just and righteous reply. My friend was unable to accept the inexplicable—to yield to the suggestion that we can never make sense intellectually of human suffering, or of personal faith, for that matter. My own background had made it difficult to explore this problem, but I understood at that moment that it was an honest and fair question and thus to be honored.

In a survey of world literature taught by a particularly inspiring and intellectual Graduate Assistant (GAs we called them) from India, I was introduced to the riches of the Orient. What I was unprepared for, however, was her carefully researched lecture on the background to the New Testament passages we had been assigned. She matter-of-factly stated that the writers of the Gospels could not have been the disciples Matthew, Mark, Luke, and John. I was dumbfounded. How could all the preachers and teachers I had listened to not dealt with this seemingly important fact? It was an evening class, I recall, and the atmosphere still lingers in my memory. We met in a tired, dingy room, the sickly yellow walls in sharp contrast to the beauty of the sari Instructor Ratna Roy was wearing. I left class that night, confused, pondering the lecture and wondering what else I had not been told by the untrained preachers at the Harrisburg Mennonite Church.

It was an assignment in a folklore class, however, that would prove particularly significant in shaping my sense of who I was. Students were encouraged to uncover stories and legends from their own backgrounds. I arranged to interview my maternal grandmother and my paternal grandfather for this assignment. My mother served as the interpreter for my deaf grandmother. I had a chance to ask about the stories I had heard from childhood and to try to sort out the relationships of the extended Stewart and Hostetler families, the deaf uncles and aunts, and where they belonged. I was particularly curious about a legend in my mother's family which dealt with a return from death, which as I learned in class was a common theme in folklore. My grandmother was able to provide the actual names and places related to this story theme in our own family.

She confirmed the account of a child who had died and was laid out, ready for burial, in a cold back room. Visitors to the house who came to pay their respects would go, as was the custom, to the back room to see the child. One of those viewing the body noticed what appeared to be slight breathing and hurriedly called the rest of the family. That child, who as I recall was identified as Rosie in our family tree, was alive and luckily restored to her parents. The spine-tingling horror of such an account lay in the speculation that any number of relatives must have been buried alive, confirmed by other childhood legends of caskets being opened, bodies exhumed, and discoveries of clawed casket lids or of a body that had turned over.

Another death story my grandmother recounted, prompted by my early memories, was of the dying child whose mother clung to him, carrying on with desperate and uncontrollable pleas. Family members, who knew death was inevitable, concluded that to allow the child to die in peace, the mother would have to be removed physically from the bedside. This accomplished, my grandmother concluded, the child died, finding rest at last.

But it was the interview with my father's father, Frank Kropf, which brought together strands of faith, fear, and awe, which transformed a pleasurable class project into something much more. The Kropf family's journey from Missouri to Oregon in an immigrant rail car and the eventual settlement in the Willamette Valley was the story my grandfather told me that day in 1972. Simply and straightforwardly, Frank outlined a family history that embodied the faith commitments of the Mennonites who settled in Oregon. My grandfather had agreed that I could tape record our conversation, a project which could not be completed in one sitting because of the marvelous detail of his recall. I had worked with my Aunt Berniece, who lived with Grandfather at the time, in arranging the interview and was pleased that she could sit in, helping interpret the questions and the memories. Some years later, Berniece transcribed the entire recording, her gift to the extended family in preserving the history of the Kropfs' settlement in the West

Frank, age eighty-five at the time of our conversation, remembered that the pacifist, German-speaking church community faced particular hardships during World War I when they refused to go to war or even to buy war bonds. Misunderstood as German sympathizers and disdained for their antiwar position, they drew unwelcome attention. Once a yellow stripe was painted around the building and the two front doors chained and padlocked. Nailed above the entrance, my grandfather recalled, was a painted sign which said, "This church is closed for the duration of the war." Although the lock was easily broken and the church reopened, the sign above the doors was left alone.

"Things went from bad to worse," Grandpa Kropf remembered. It was 1918 and the Mennonites' refusal to purchase "victory bonds" fed the irritation of the community. Rowdies, as my grandfather called them, sometimes drove around late at night scaring families by shooting off guns. "I think I could show you the marks on the walls yet where the bullets scraped the walls," Frank said.

Things came to a head one day when two carloads of "young husky fellows" showed up at several places in the Mennonite settlement, including my grandfather's and great grandfather's place. Grandpa recalled that his father "surmised at once what was plain, that it was a mob. Of course, you don't argue with them and you don't say more than you absolutely have to." Nothing happened then, but later that evening a carload returned to my grandfather's place since he had been gone when they had stopped earlier in the day. I can still hear my grandfather's voice—I can still see him sitting in his customary rocking chair—recounting the particulars of that night:

"When I came home in the evening, Mom said what had happened and she said they said they'd be back again this evening. She had supper ready, so we ate, and getting about sundown here they came. Just one car came. One big husky fellow got out and the others stayed in the car. He came to the fence, I was on the inside, and he wanted to know why we don't want to fight for the war. Well, I said, we don't believe in killing other people. And so he said, 'If someone would molest your wife, you'd fight!' All I said was, 'If there's any killing to be done, somebody else will have to do the killing.' That's all I said. The Lord gave me what to say.

"He jumped in the car and said, 'If that's the way you feel about it, you'll have to take the consequences,' and just zoomed out of here like the devil was after him. Now how would you feel going to bed when they talk like that? Well, we came in, had family worship and put the children to bed. We just committed ourselves to the Lord, whatever we'd have, He'd take care of it. We went to bed and went to sleep and they never came back."

What Frank went on to say was even more startling and did not follow the legend theme we were studying in my folklore course at the university. The postscript to the story is what my grandfather learned much later: "Only a few years ago, I found out why they didn't carry out their plans. They were prepared and ready to take us out and tar and feather us, but when they came there was a heavenly being that stood between them and us and they couldn't get a hold of anybody. . . . One of the fellows said this many years later. Just a few years ago—not over five years ago, I found it out. The angel of the Lord encampeth round about those that fear Him."

There the story rests, later to be passed on to my siblings and cousins, to their children and grandchildren, and to my two daughters and their children—a testimony of faith from generation to generation. Looking out the south window toward the church house that day as I listened to his voice, I could almost see the painted yellow stripe still encircling the church. Seven years later, my grandfather died at age 92.

✛

The Man in the Stacks

An unexpected encounter at the university seems in retro-spect one of those moments out of time which gathers up the ghosts of childhood and transforms memory into a re-deemable past. But, as a mature woman in my forties, I was not there yet, as I discovered in the university library perusing the stacks for a particular book. It was a dim section of the library, which could suggest, perhaps, some doubt about what or who I saw. There in the narrow aisle between high metal shelves of books was an old man, dressed in overalls. I recognized him. Suddenly I was the seven-year-old with pigtails back on the farm. I froze. I have no memory of how long I stood there, of whether I stared unable to take in what I was seeing. Heart thumping in my chest, waves of fear and shock hitting me cold, I turned and walked away.

Why was he there? How could he be there? Then reason began to return and I reassured myself that at least he would not have recognized me. I left the library. The next moments are blank, but I imagine that I must have needed desperately to get out into the fresh air, to give myself distance, to be with people as protection from the man in the stacks. That he was now old and no longer a threat I knew with my head, but I could not control the child's terror.

The summer of 1948 when our new house was being built, I must have been underfoot often, following my dad around, playing in some corner out of the way of the construction crew. I was prone to obey and trust anyone, so I was not prepared when one of the workmen instructed me one day to go to the barn and he would come. There was no hint of danger, since this was not a stranger. And so I followed instructions. Worse than the violation of innocence was the need to keep the secret—which he ordered me to do. And so I was doubly harmed, by the act itself and by the necessity of carrying alone a burden of guilt.

As it turned out, the encounter in the stacks proved to be a release. I had faced the man who had wronged me. The years of childhood sleeplessness, sifting through guilt and unbearable aloneness, suddenly yielded to a sense that the past was now redeemed. Over the years as I gradually realized what had happened to me, I thought I would surely be prohibited from marrying. Then the adolescent maturation process overrode the child's skewed view of what would be expected of me and I fell in love. The seven-year-old's promise to keep a secret now seemed negotiable. I would confess to my fiancée, when the time came, what had happened. Confiding in my husband-to-be took me a great way through the healing process and, for the most part, I could put the secret wound behind me. Sometimes I convince myself that the childhood episode gave me a strength I would not otherwise have possessed.

The sadness I feel is for the child that suffered from an anguish borne in silence with no possibility of being granted absolution by a parent or a teacher or a minister who could have said, "It's not your fault." Over the years, I learned something about grace and the way that faith sustains us even in the face of evil. But it was not until that day in the University of Oregon library that the inner fear which had no name was finally exorcised. I knew that it no longer had power over me.

There were balancing joys of childhood, though, which compensated for the shadow experiences and I emerged relatively healthy into adulthood. One was an unlikely friendship with a Polish refugee couple who was sponsored by my grandparents. The couple lived in a tiny house on my grandparents' farm. I loved to go with my parents to visit George and Luda Mantusz, particularly to see George who gave me full attention and made me feel special. His charm and love of life were contagious. When George and Luda named their first child Lela—my name—I felt singled out and, even as a five or six-year-old, understood that this was a great honor.

I am still intrigued by names and do not fully understand the impulses that steer us in one direction or another in the identities we assume. I was aware growing up that I was named for my father's sister Lela who died of diphtheria at age seven. To my mother, I am still Lela Fern. I have one aunt by the same name. My mother-in-law always called me just Lela. It was in high school that my close friends began calling me Lee and gradually that was the name I came to feel most comfortable with. Later, in administrative roles that were more traditionally held by males, I would get a perverse pleasure out of receiving letters addressed to Mr. Lee Snyder. Occasionally, I would be introduced to someone who knew me only by name and would be clearly taken aback at being presented to a woman. I confess, that reaction was also strangely satisfying.

+

Just Say Yes

Identity, fate, destiny, providence, luck—these represent a constellation of terms for powers that shape and guide us. In my experience, these inscrutable forces unfold with no small amount of mystery. Do we discover or create our destiny? We do both and sometimes, in retrospect, we glimpse patterns that guide us. I did not understand that for a long time, seeing myself as incredibly lucky. I had a wonderful life partner, daughters who taught me much along the way, and opportunities for study and work. I had a healthy appreciation for providence—for God's calling on my life—but I was mostly content to view my life as one in which God every so often interrupted the normal flow.

It was embarrassing, actually, this belief that I was handed these incredible and surprise opportunities. I felt undeserving and was not always certain I was fully prepared for the challenges. It gradually began to dawn on me that the patterns I had observed in my parents—willingness to take risks, saying "yes" to the church, and demonstrating openness to uncertain possibilities—was a legacy that had become a part of me. My husband (who saw things the same way) and I pursued the future almost unconsciously out of the perspective and values we had seen in our parents.

The poets often see and say what we have yet to understand on a conscious level. So it was another poet who crystallized for me the realization that I had had more to do with my life trajectory than I had given myself credit for. "Say Yes Quickly," by a California writer with the sensibilities of my own Mennonite upbringing explained a lot.

> Say yes quickly, before you think too hard
> or the soles of your feet give out.
> Say yes before you see the to-do list.
> Saying maybe will only get you to the door,
> but never past it.
> Say yes before the dove departs for, yes,
> she will depart and you will be left
> alone with your yes,
> your affirmation of what you
> couldn't possibly know was coming . . .
> Keep saying yes.
> —Sherri Hostetler, *A Cappella: Mennonite Voices in Poetry*

That's it, I thought, when I discovered Sherri's poem. My whole life I have been saying yes.

PART FOUR

FINDING THE WAY

✠

Keeping Things Straight

Lists have always served me well. My mother made lists too. They seemed a regular part of keeping things straight. Grocery lists, lists of jobs to do, maybe a few cryptic notes ordering the week. I have learned to keep track of myself by making lists more or less any old time, often in my journal. Just writing down what has contributed to the mounting sense of chaos at the office or noting the schedule ahead offers the illusion, at least, of being in control. My whirling-dervish tendencies are thus tamed and I calm myself, reminded that the one-thing-at-a-time approach usually works.

For example, I find this list in my journal, pulling together the threads of a particularly wearying week—the week President Bush declared war on Iraq. "While the world tilts into deeper chaos, the sanity of daily routine becomes one's salvation" (March 22, 2003). And then the list—a president's typical schedule:

- MEA meetings conclude Saturday
- Linda and her family visit Saturday afternoon
- Athletic Awards dinner Saturday night
- Sunday, Camarata concert and senior art reception
- Sunday night, basketball awards dinner
- Monday, luncheon honoring the volunteers
- Tuesday, a.m., hospital committee meeting in Findlay
- Tuesday, travel to Sidney to make an OFIC corporation contact
- Wednesday, brown-bag lunch for the university discussion

- Wednesday, retirees coffee
- Thursday, another brown-bag lunch to continue the university forum
- Thursday, early evening—candlelight service at First Mennonite
- Thursday, later—campus service in response to the war declaration
- Friday, President's Council of Corporate Advisors
- Friday, President's "Occasional Friday" discussion
- Next week: faculty meeting, host MSEC dinner, Cabinet, reception for Don Neuen, head out Thursday for Michigan conference, return late Saturday night
- Sunday, the finale of the Bach Festival; Neuen conducts the *Elijah*.

On a September morning before College Hall awakens, I spend a few minutes with my journal, trying to stave off a vague sense of foreboding and dread. It is a wet Monday. There are budget challenges, an unhappy faculty member, and grapevine irritations. Nothing unusual about those. I know it is only the work that will save me and proceed to jot down the tasks:

- Finalize the President's Society letter
- Confirm the George Rable invitation for November 15
- Send the Advancement Committee the Ray Ramseyer Award nomination
- Prepare for the conference call tomorrow morning with the board chair
- Outline assignments agreed to with the Vice President for Advancement
- Call two alumni donors
- Complete plans for the meeting of the Council of Church Leaders
- Three appointments today

Then I hear my assistant come into the outer office. I listen to her start up her computer, unlock the bolt on the side door, and drop her shoes to the hard plastic floor mat as she changes into office pumps. Against these reassuring sounds, the day takes shape. I am ready for the week.

In recalling the surprises and convergences in this journey I call my life, at times I find myself second-guessing the chronology of events. Why do I recall, upon returning from Nigeria in summer 1968, that we watched the moon landing sitting around the television with cousins in their living room? So clear was this memory that I was surprised to discover much later that Neil Armstrong's moon walk was in 1969, not 1968. Maybe a one-year discrepancy shouldn't matter, I tell myself. Or was I remembering the Apollo 7 launch?

Nevertheless, that lapse in memory gives me pause, and I wonder how one reconciles such disparities. Maybe, as Jean-Paul Sartre observed, memory is a construction, not a retrieval.

So, just as I attempt to center my focus and stave off confusion by making lists, I sketch a time line, trying to make sense of it all. So far this seems to cover the bare facts, although it is mostly an exercise to remind myself that the past, while created out of what passes for reality, is incomplete and sometimes inaccurate.

A Chronology

1940: Lela Fern Kropf, oldest of six, is born to Lloyd and Ruth Stewart Kropf at Harrisburg, Oregon, on December 12.

1952: Moved to California at age eleven, where the family lives for six years, involved in the work of the Sacramento Rock of Ages Rescue Mission.

1956: Enrolled at Western Mennonite School, Salem, Oregon, as a sophomore boarding student. Graduated from WMS in 1959.

1959: Engaged to Delbert W. Snyder. Attended Eastern Mennonite College for one year, 1959-60.

1960: Married at Albany, Oregon, July 29.

1960-63: Moved to Eugene, Oregon, for Delbert to continue university studies. First daughter, Lori, born 1961. Second daughter, Judith, born 1962.

1963-65: Moved to Portland where Delbert taught high school mathematics upon completion of his master's program. Repaid college loans and explored international service options.

1965-68: Accepted a Mennonite Board of Missions overseas appointment, teaching at the Qua Ibo Secondary School, Etinan, East Nigeria. Three-year assignment interrupted by the Biafran War. Relocated to Northern Nigeria (Jos) for the final year of teaching.

1968-69: Moved to Portland, Oregon, where Delbert taught at Madison High School.

1969-72: Returned to Eugene to the University of Oregon, Delbert to pursue doctoral studies and Lee to resume undergraduate work.

1971-72: Graduated from the university mid-year with a B.A. in English; continued with graduate courses. Phi Beta Kappa and Mortar Board honors.

1972: The family moved to Harrisonburg, Virginia, for Delbert's appointment in mathematics at Eastern Mennonite College.

1972-74: Enrolled in graduate studies at James Madison University, along with a teaching assistantship. Received an M.A. in English Literature and Linguistics 1974.

1974-82: Accepted an assignment in the Academic Dean's Office, Eastern Mennonite College (administrative assistant, assistant to the dean, assistant dean), while teaching part-time.

1982-84: Returned to the West Coast for a two-year sabbatical/professional leave for doctoral studies at the University of Oregon. Completed comprehensive examinations and received approval for proposed dissertation.

1984-85: Appointed as interim Academic Dean, Eastern Mennonite College. Upon completion of the dissertation, May 1985, received a Ph.D. in English Literature.

1985-96: Served as Vice-President and Dean of Academic Affairs, Eastern Mennonite University.

1996: Took office as eighth president of (then) Bluffton College, Bluffton, Ohio.

2006: Completed ten years as president, Bluffton University, retiring in Harrisonburg, Virginia; also resides part of the year in Salem, Oregon.

A chronology is straightforward, so free of clutter, so apparently simple. It helps sort out the tangles of fact and memory, as I try to make sense of it all. And yet life is more complicated than that.

✛

Learning My Mother's Language

It is said that remembering is an act of the imagination, and I have no reason to doubt it. I have come to understand that memory's intuition offers a truth of its own, enlarging and extending life in some inexplicable way. At least that is the case in my relationship with my mother and our complicated patterns of communication.

On one level, we shared an easy camaraderie, an unprovoked and respectful form of exchange based on the ordinary interests of Mennonite farm women. We kept track of things, exchanged gossip, commented on church and family news, and noted the passage of time through deaths, births, and community tragedies. Even as an adult, I found it difficult to shuck the daughter role. I did not need to, nor did I want to. After my dad died, when my mother would travel from Oregon to visit us in Ohio or Virginia, I would wonder fleetingly if there was the possibility of a new conversation, more intimate, outside the worn grooves of familiar roles. In our community the women kept their inner lives private. None of this modern day mother-daughter psychologizing where disappointments are aired or long buried hurts are hurled at one another.

There was another level of communication, however, that was so pervasively obvious that for years I was not attuned to its significance. I remember it only as my mother's preoccupation with the weather. This was not simply a matter of passing interest or the topic of casual conversation. For her, the weather was more like a beloved reassuring presence. Not having TV, our family did not have the ubiquitous weather channel to signal the week's forecast. The radio announcer kept us periodically informed of the temperature and the measure of rainfall, but it was the barometer that was given a favored place in our house. There the mysterious black box with its three instrument panels sat on the fireplace mantel beside the dark wood-encased chime clock which called out the hours and the half hours.

Sometimes during the day, when my mother would sense a subtle atmospheric shift, she would check the barometer and announce, "The barometer's up." Or, "The barometer's down." My father would give the device a tap just before going to bed, preparing himself for whatever weather change would order the next day's work. I never did understand the barometer's pressure gauges or how the floating hands of the meters conveyed real weather information, but they made perfect sense to my mom and dad.

My mother seemed to possess an expanded sense of weather, as something beyond the ordinary, an expression of both an inner and outer state of being. I have learned from my mother to see and feel, to hear and fear the weather. To hope and marvel, to taste and touch the wind or the sharp edge of a March morning. I can still see Mom bracing herself against the gusts, hanging out the bath towels and the overalls on the backyard clothesline next to the grape arbor.

When each Saturday I call my mother, now in her nineties, in the retirement village, she asks, "What's the weather like there?" We exchange reports on an infinite variety of weather manifestations and shifts—interminable rain, a heavy freeze, the warm fog, the first snowfall. Or it might be the Shenandoah's fall blaze and Oregon's extended Indian summer. "It was forty degrees this morning," she says, or fifty or maybe sixty-three. Some days she takes a walk, depending on the weather. I imagine her bundled in a favorite ratty brown sweater, hunched against the wind as she follows the sidewalk around Quail Run. (I know she has gotten rid of that sweater by this time, but I indulge the memory of her hanging on to worn dresses, old jackets and sagging coats, because that is my own tendency.)

My mother's letters over the years, when she still found pleasure in writing and before Parkinson's frustrated her worn and nimble hands, have always revealed two things: her faith and her love for the rhythms of the year. "Greetings in Jesus' name," her letters would begin. Then she would move into an account of the week's activities: the boys fertilizing the field, planting the garden, spraying, windrowing, harvesting. After heavy spring rains, she would report that the creek's been up—or back down. Sometimes she would register a strong north wind or "skiff" of snow. There was something comforting about her litany of duties: raking leaves, cutting out quilt blocks for the women's sewing circle, going to Wednesday night prayer meeting, mowing the yard and orchard. But always there was the weather. "It's dry," she would write. "The farmers really need rain." Or, just as often, "The fields are so wet that the boys can't get in to cut the fescue."

While still on the farm, she used to write about February daffodils which bloomed in their wildness along the fence rows or in the ditches along the road and about the early camellias outside the dining room window. This was the prize *Floribunda,* I would remember, an astonishingly large pink specimen which served as a harbinger of the coming of spring. "I picked a bouquet of daffodils where the old shed used to be," Mom would write, and I pictured exactly where she had gathered them.

Even with experience and a keen eye for reading the skies, my mother acknowledged—perhaps longed for—the unpredictable and disruptive chaos of weather which served as a manifestation of life itself. Omni-present, the weather was a force to be reckoned with. She knew this without ever having heard of weather modeling, chaos theory, and Edward Lorenz's question, "Does the flap of a butterfly's wing in Brazil set off a tornado in Texas?" She would have opted to observe cloud patterns and sunsets firsthand rather than consider theories of whether the Butterfly Effect magnifies small uncertainties into large-scale weather phenomena.

Weather was more than just a daily companion, however. It took me a long time to understand that weather is code language for my mother. I am still learning the language, but I know when she asks me, "How's the weather?" that she is really asking, "How are you doing?" "Are you okay?" As a farm woman inextricably linked to the land, Mom's sense of order and change, of possibility and wonder, is expressed through the language of weather. Some Saturdays I press her, "And how are you, Mom?" "Oh, about the same," she replies, adding more only if I insist. And so we talk about the weather, which gives us permission to address the soul while acknowledging chaos and predictability, mystery and surprise, expectations of the moment—and hopes for tomorrow.

✢

Laundry and Other Mysteries

If much of my upbringing could not have predicted the work
which I would eventually embrace, there were what I would
call the "basics" which provided a solid foundation for what lay
ahead: love of family, the daily example of my parents' faith, de-
votion to the church, and a commonsense, humble reverence
for work. My father's books, insatiable curiosity, and love of
learning were undeniably key in my own development. But my
mother's more understated virtues of appreciating the commonplace, of thriving in the repetitive tasks of household matters, of facing the unexpected with fortitude and faith, were
equally significant.

When my sister and I ask our mother about her struggle
with polio, she sketches only the merest details—the doctor
consultations, the difficulty in diagnosing her mysterious condition, and then, finally, the physician who concludes that she
is suffering from infantile paralysis. As mother of a baby and a
toddler, how did she manage as she fought her way back to full
health? Who took care of us, my sister and me, I wonder? Only
when we probe does my mother say more about the long recovery, the hot water baths prescribed for treatment—baths she
took down at my grandparents' place since they had hot running water and a real bath tub.

But it was the uneventful, daily routines which mostly carried us along. It is difficult to fathom how rich is such a ground-
ing in the ordinary, so I seize on the words of others who have
found a way to say it. I rediscover a brief journal notation from
reading I had forgotten: "The mundane—the stuff of our

lives—is irreplaceable," I noted, "essential, eternal and changing, beautiful and fearsome, beyond human understanding, worthy of reverence and awe" (Sept. 29, 2004). My mother and I did not talk like this in real life, but it was a deep knowledge we shared. From her I learned to love the fixtures of everyday life. I learned to love the laundry—the wordless incantations of cleansing and renewal. We would gather in from the clothesline the dry towels and sheets, burying our faces in a cool fragrance more heavenly than any of those spring-scented laundry products. The drudgery of doing the dishes or ironing was another matter, but Mom claimed even to enjoy washing dishes—a job we girls wished she would just do, if she liked it so much.

In retrospect, I recognize the near physical pleasure derived in the simple satisfactions of a clean house. The anticipation of reading a book after the "Saturday's work" was done taught me the value of delayed gratification; do the job as quickly as possible but take pride in the work. Do it well, and then reward yourself. I learned also that the tedium of work can yield a variety of pleasures. While dusting and vacuuming on a Saturday morning, I would stack several LPs on the turntable of the large RCA in the living room and lose myself in the music. Even with the limited selection of records my folks had accumulated, I had my favorites: Edvard Grieg's *Peer Gynt Suites* and Tchaikovsky's *1812 Overture*.

The mean and ordinary rigors of running a household provided a primer for how to get things done without fuss. I learned that being practical is an honorable discipline and that humility in all things is God's command. What I was surprised to discover much later, in the messiness of human relationships and office pressures, is how well the old habits of housework would serve.

One day I received a letter from an angry and unusually articulate constituent of the college. It was filled with such venom and bile that I could think of only one thing to do. Whatever the intended message, it was a personal attack. I needed to settle myself down, having never before—or since—received a letter like that one. I went home and cleaned the toilets. I confess, I later destroyed the letter, an action of slight regret now. Could it have been that bad, I wonder?

In recalling certain decision points in my life, I notice the curious juxtaposition of the mundane—"women's work"—with what turned out to be extraordinary interruptions to the commonplace. I recall the muggy day I was on my hands and knees scrubbing a worn turquoise carpet left behind in a little house we had bought. The telephone rang. I was deep in the suds, hoping to revitalize the old wool rug. Drying off my hands, I picked up the phone and was taken aback to hear the assistant to the college president asking if I would consider an opening in the dean's office instead of the job I had already accepted in another office at Eastern Mennonite.

I have come to associate interruptions and surprise with the everyday matters of housekeeping. The next such call came while I was doing the laundry. It was 1995, the year Del and I had decided it was time to explore other career possibilities. We had not gotten so far as to pursue particular positions. We both had rewarding, though all-consuming, work. We sensed, however, that it was time for a change.

That Saturday in August when the phone rang, I stepped out of the laundry room and picked up the basement extension. Our friend Ed Diller was on the line, but the noise from the washing machine made it difficult to hear why he was calling. I finally had the good sense to excuse myself and shut off the washer, learning only later that this was not a call from just the board chair and the head of the Bluffton presidential search committee, but that a number of other committee members were listening in as well. Later folding towels and matching socks, I found the routines of the laundry a near perfect way to focus the mad scramble of questions as I thought about Ed's call.

The Woman Question

I would have had difficulty explaining to any number of those who have influenced my life the deep-rooted attractions of the everyday, whether they be the chores of the household or my mother's contentment in the role of "helpmeet," a term that I associate with wedding ceremonies in childhood and with all those instructions about woman's place. I realize with some astonishment, as I observe feminist friends and mentors, that for some inexplicable reason, I have been spared the poisonous discontents that are often associated with a strict insistence on women's subordinate role. I cannot explain why, but the traditional woman's place did not diminish my sense of possibility.

Professor Johnson would not have understood that at all. In the early 1970s, feminists had taken center stage at the university, along with other activists. It was an intoxicating and sometimes frightening time. Prince Lucien Campbell, which housed the English Department, was bombed. Classes were disrupted by war protesters in combat fatigues brandishing guns and simulating violence by positioning "bodies" in classroom doorways. Everyone, it seemed, had their favorite cause. My Chaucer professor, who was of the women's lib bra-burning stripe, dramatized her own commitments by announcing one day in class that she was not going to march up three flights in Fenton Hall, the law building where English classes were sometimes scheduled, to find the ladies restroom.

When the law school was designed, it was assumed that all students would be served by a first-floor men's room. Professor

Mary Ann Johnson took great pleasure in making her point by using the men's lavatory.

That summer, the class studied Middle English literature and the marvels of the *Canterbury Tales*. We were introduced also to the politics of gender and were amazed to discover that the characters of a medieval text could be so contemporary—at least through the interpretive lens of the instructor. The fact is that my passionate, bra-less professor looms larger in memory than any of the lively pilgrims of Chaucer's tales.

While I did not always identify with the tactics of the feminists on campus, Ms. Johnson's lessons were not lost on me. I understood that this movement signaled a new day for women. I recalled the Chaucer restroom mini-drama when we got to Eastern Mennonite for Del's teaching job. I learned that the EMC science center was as outdated as the University of Oregon law school. On the floor where the laboratories and faculty offices were located in the science building, the only restroom was designated for men. About the time we arrived in summer 1972, a plan was underway to turn a large science center cloakroom into a women's restroom. It was high time, for the sciences were no longer the purview of just male students and male faculty members.

Speaking and Silence

Symbolically and literally, women were finding their voices in the early '70s. It was a heady time at the university, but to those of us who were neither angry nor obsessed with gaining some imagined freedom, it was perhaps too easy to stand on the sidelines watching the theatrics. It was a selfish view, in many ways. I had all the freedom I wanted, being able to complete college with the full support and encouragement of husband and daughters. I was also just beginning to come to terms with my early conditioning that women were destined for a private sphere and were expected to keep silent.

I have lived much of my life with an affliction—maybe disability is a better term—the burden of needing to speak and being unable to speak. This was more than simply not having the right words. Early in the deanship at Eastern Mennonite, long after the time when women were excluded from administrative positions, on public occasions when I needed to sit on the high auditorium stage, I would suffer something close to vertigo if I were seated too close to the edge. Overcome by an irrational fear of falling off the platform, I would adjust my chair as unobtrusively as possible to gain just a few inches of security.

The necessity of being a public person in the roles in which I have found myself has been a challenging road. The sick-in-the-stomach wrenching in final preparations for whatever presentation or address I was giving took me years to overcome. There was always the near crisis of needing to start over, the overwhelming impulse to discard the whole thing when it was too late. This resulted in a sort of doomed resignation that I had to do what I had to do, whether or not I had chosen the wrong subject or had committed some error in judgment as I crafted my speech.

I learned to overcome these self-revulsions and to find a way not to let them overwhelm me. Sometimes I blame Bud Baker. Maybe I should say, I thank Bud Baker. When I was five years old, I had a speaking part in the summer Bible school program at the little Harrisburg Mennonite Church there at the corner of Powerline and Diamond Hill Road. I loved Bible school— the songs, the stories, the workbooks, the cutouts. The final night of the program was a big deal. Farmers would clean up from being in the fields. The men would put on their Sunday white shirts and the women would change from their everyday clothes to Sunday capes.

I cannot remember my assigned verse that night, but I do recall that it was a solemn privilege to speak aloud in front of the congregation—men and boys seated on the left and the women on the right. Nervous and excited, I spoke too fast and too quietly. "We couldn't hear you." That was Bud Baker's complaint. A friend of my parents, this jovial, ruddy-cheeked man had noticed my part in the program and he spoke to me afterward. They were chiding and joking words. Possibly meant as encouragement, his comment was devastating. I wanted to be silent the rest of my life.

That fortunate or unfortunate assessment had an effect on me; it does not matter that it was only a remark to a child on a hot summer evening. That memory, along with the subtle or not so subtle conditioning all the girls of the church received that taught us that women were not to speak in public, remain a part of my psyche. My greatest fear when asked to be academic dean was whether I could speak in public—a necessary part of the role. There is almost no way to describe the depths of what seems on the face of it to be such a petty fear.

✣

Finding the Way

It was a time of exhaustion, exhilaration, and sometimes excruciating decisions in my new role as dean. Back at Eastern Mennonite College, I was finding my way in an unfamiliar public role. The trustees had mandated a reduction of program and staff to stabilize the finances of the institution. In addition to the fiscal challenges, I would be writing my dissertation on the weekends. On the first morning that I made my way to the dean's office, down a long hallway through the quiet dimness because it was very early, I was suddenly overcome by the sense that I had no business being there. I was an imposter. The moment passed and I laughed, realizing that sneaking into my new office was ludicrous.

Near the end of my University of Oregon sabbatical, when the EMU president had called me asking if I would allow my name to be considered as academic dean, I had said no. I knew the demands of the office because I had worked for several deans, honorable men who taught me much. I knew that there was never enough money and, no matter how dedicated were my wonderful colleagues, there would always be unhappy faculty, petty concerns, and a few making unreasonable demands. I knew too much, actually, about the inner workings of the office.

But the president persisted. The telephone rang in our Eugene student apartment. It was the president again, reporting that the faculty was asking me to reconsider. I knew that I had loved my work as assistant dean and that a nobility of purpose and a commitment to service were at the heart of the educational enterprise. I had experienced that incomparable sense of satisfaction when a messy problem yields an unexpected solution or when the teaching-learning exchange reveals transformative powers. I had worked alongside amazing faculty and had been mentored by some of the best administrators I would ever know.

The return from graduate school to a new position was a journey again being played out in my subconscious. It was as though I could relinquish to some inner guide whatever needed attending to. Most of this was of the usual sort—silly dream collages of people and places—the stuff one promptly forgets on waking. Some of these dreams, however, insisted on an appearance in the conscious realm. They were startlingly magnificent and recurred in variations of color and calm, charged with energy yet filled with an indescribable peace. These dreams evoked images of fire and ice, of mountain passes and cool greens, of steamy tropics and lush growth. In this parallel realm, a broad ribbon of highway stretched miles and miles up the mountain toward the blue heights—this time the journey was exhilarating, the snow caps brilliant. Here and there grassy meadows offered refreshment.

Back down that highway, the road descends quickly to a tropical place somewhere out of time. There is a sense of great speed traveling the winding road as it narrows and rounds with sudden entrance into a totally different locale. In contrast to whites and greens and blues, this is a place of vibrant warmth, of sensuous closeness, of teeming life. There are people here, but no one recognizable. These dreamscapes have become real places to me. They offer a retreat into the mystery of connections which mostly lie submerged in that part of one's being which attends to the spirit and soul.

Scattered now and then across a mostly reasoned and reasonable life, these nightscapes have served as great gifts—renderings of some larger vision that perhaps I could have gained from the philosophers twenty-five years earlier as a student, had I been ready. As an academic I am suspicious of dreams. I have never studied Freud, and I tend to be skeptical about dreams being the key to anything. So, I keep being surprised at the convergence of these dazzling subconscious images with everyday encounters, as I was in discovering a reference to Ralph Waldo Emerson in a book on leadership. Margaret Wheatley, writing about *Leadership and the New Science,* notes Emerson's view of life as an ongoing encounter with the unknown and singles out this passage: "We wake and find ourselves on a stair; there are stairs below us which we seem to have ascended, there are stairs above us which go out of sight."

With amazement, I recognized this very image. I began to understand that we have access to an unbidden realm which helps us make sense of our lives. Emerson's stairway was a variant of my own experience. Lest this seem total nonsense, allow me to explain.

✠

Convergences—the Ascending Stairs

While I had worked through the essays of Ralph Waldo Emerson back in the early 1980s in Dr. Griffith's seminar, I did not remember the image of the suspended stairway. I can scarcely describe the effect of stumbling on this reference. Why? Because, just when I was reading Wheatley, one of the leadership gurus of the time, a journal had crossed my desk—the full-color cover sketch a striking rendition of an ascending stairs. This rendering showed a figure mounting a suspended flight of steps—a great staircase arising out of blue depths and ascending into obscured heights. I recognized the imagery, which evoked the memory of another dream I had had of speeding into the turn of a great curved highway, stretching up and out into space—then disappearing into the ether. That dream had combined a heightened sense of great speed and exhilaration with the terrifying sensation of literally flying off into space.

I am still skittish even talking about dreams. But the convergence of images in my chance readings—readings that served to heighten the impact of a similar dream—proved irresistible. I had to search out the original Emerson passage, which I finally found in his essay, "Experience."

Picking up Wheatley and rediscovering Emerson at the very same time that the magazine cover showed up in my mail was at the very least astonishing. But not, in my experience, all that unusual. I am not the first to notice, as someone once said, that "By an agency that is not coincidence . . . we find, and are found by, the books we need to enlarge and complete us." This is simply the recognition that in the intersections and connections that make up our experience—in this case words and images—there is some mystery that we need to pay attention to. I am learning to notice.

I am also learning to welcome the unexpected. I can only stand in awe of the way our lives unfold. Unbidden, the old night terrors give way to the freedom and energy of new dreams. I understand more about faith and fallibility as one's inner consciousness sorts it all out. With gratitude, I continue to find my way, welcoming the joy of beauty and surprise.

PART FIVE

SEASONS OF THE PRESIDENCY

✛

The Accidental President

"God, is this strange or what?" I was beginning the fourth
year of the presidency at Bluffton University. This is the
question that forced itself on me as I considered the unfolding
surprises of the past several years, pressed by the sense that I had
been drawn into a stream of action not by my own choosing. I
had never imagined myself a college president. Nor could I have
fully anticipated, in the glow of the campus welcome and the
festivities of the inauguration ceremonies, what immediately
lay ahead.

By the end of my first month in office, the academic dean,
who was my mainstay and a highly regarded leader of the faculty, informed me of his diagnosis of cancer. To undergo treatment and to help recovery, the dean requested an extended
leave which led, before the end of the year, to his decision to retire—a profoundly sad development for all of us.

In my tentative understandings of a new position in an unfamiliar place, I had counted on the wisdom and experience of
my colleague to ensure a smooth leadership transition. Now I
had to resist the temptation to step in and simply pick up the
pieces, to take on the dean's work, a job I knew well. Realizing
that I needed to concentrate on my own responsibilities, I
quickly discovered that I could rely fully on the administrative
team and on faculty leaders to help a novice president find the
way.

The first year in the presidency concluded with an unlikely
convergence of events: The commencement speaker died a few
days before his scheduled appearance and the outdoor gradua-

tion ceremony was rained out. Flash floods created a mess on campus. In those early months in the president's office, I would discover something about the sheer unpredictability of the job. I would learn more also about the courage and faith of the college community.

By July the following year (1998), the campus would be plunged into the first of two crises which unfolded in short order. A summer band camp was underway, drawing high school students from around the region. Late morning on a Friday at the end of July, the relentless wail of sirens began to seep into the consciousness of those of us working at our desks in College Hall. The word came shortly. Scaffolding erected for use by the band director had collapsed on the practice field. An unknown number of students had also been on the scaffolding, and there were serious injuries.

Emergency teams from surrounding counties and towns poured in. Under the noon sun, rescue workers attended to those involved, arranging to airlift the most seriously injured. The network television corps also descended. Hovering overhead in their helicopters and arriving in vans, the reporters saw this accident as a primetime extension of the just-released national news exposé of the dangers of scaffolding. A small campus in a tiny Midwest town was unaccustomed to the media frenzy, but that was the least of the community's concerns as medics, pastors, counselors, and campus personnel attended to the victims and to their families. When it was eventually determined that there would be no fatalities, the news teams soon directed their attention to other stories, including that afternoon's shooting at the nation's Capitol in Washington, D.C.

Two months later the campus would be shaken by a dormitory fire, with fourteen students injured, one seriously. It was before dawn when the telephone in our bedroom rang. The residence director, with a strained urgency in her voice, reported that there was a fire in Ropp Hall. There was little time for reflection in the hours and days following. The college women were reassigned to other halls and clean-up began. While officials undertook a systematic investigation into the cause of the fire, traumatized students sought comfort by returning to campus routines. Arson was the investigators' conclusion. Within a short time an arrest had been made; a student was taken into custody and then even more questions emerged. How, in a safe and beloved community, could this happen? Why?

The aftermath of the residence hall fire required much time and energy over the next weeks and months. Insurance issues, lawsuits, depositions, fact finding, and a host of complexities resulting from both the scaffolding accident and the fire consumed enormous staff energy. But other matters were pressing. News of a foundation grant to support the construction of an academic center had just arrived. While this was good news, it was still necessary to meet with the architects and contractor to further reduce projected building costs. Enrollment had dipped, so the year's operating budget required adjustment.

I was preparing to leave for a Wellesley conference on "Education as Transformation" and, at the same time, suffering from poison oak. Just several days after the Ropp Hall fire, I had gone to my office in the early dawn, hoping in the quietness to gain perspective and strength for whatever might be ahead. Outside, the campus lights along the walkways were still burning. There was a knock at the outer office door. Startled, I greeted Nan, the assistant campus pastor, hesitant about interrupting. She announced that she wanted to pray with me.

Nan's obedience to an impulse carried me through the day, and I embraced a sense both of total inadequacy and wonder at God's working. I was reminded of the Old Testament account of Moses, in the Israelites' skirmish with the Amalekites, standing on a hill holding up his hands to God while the battle waged around him. As long as the leader's arms were raised to the heavens, the Israelites were winning. But Moses could not keep this up all day; he got tired and it became necessary for two of the elders to hold up Moses' arms to assure success in the fight. There were many times I knew that my arms were being held up by the strength of others.

The Lady of Laughter

One of the delights of the presidency as I began to get a feel for the flow of the work was learning to know a company of characters from Bluffton's past and present who maintained connections to the college. There were the encouragers, sometimes the naysayers, the saints who prayed for me regularly, the community leaders who generously shared their advice and support. These folks, who had known Bluffton College much longer than I, regaled me with awesome tales and fascinating histories. Through very personal reminiscences, they revealed the transformative power of their experience at a small, unpretentious campus spanning Little Riley Creek amid corn and soybean fields.

At one of my first alumni gatherings, an old-timer told me with tears in his eyes of Bluffton giving him a "second chance." On the verge of being expelled because of failing grades, this student was rescued by President Robert Kreider, who decided he should be given another opportunity. That decision, the alumnus told me, had changed his life.

As Bluffton's eighth president, I had the eminently good fortune to draw on the knowledge and expertise of three predecessors who were available to me when I needed them. But I also found a mentor in the most unlikely place: Hollywood. Phyllis Diller, comedienne and musician, was of an earlier generation. Phyllis Driver had arrived on campus before I was born, enrolling as a student in 1939 after several years studying music in Chicago. On a trip west to visit alumni and to meet Bluffton supporters, I received a warm welcome from this now-famous performer. She invited me to her home just off Sunset Boulevard for lunch.

We hit it off from the start, comparing our rural backgrounds and Virginia connections. She was one of the Shenandoah Valley Drivers, she told me, and showed me a photo of her Dunkard preacher grandfather. She took great pleasure in giving me a tour of the house—the offices, the "wig room," the costume collection, two art studios, and her bedroom. We laughed when we discovered that we both eat popcorn in bed. She insisted, however, that a certain brand of chocolate soda was an essential accompaniment and wrapped two cans for me in a brown paper bag to take home.

Her house was filled with mementos and celebrity photos. Framed pictures of Hollywood friends and notables crowded the top of the grand piano in the front parlor. When we came to what she called "the pump room," she agreed to sit down and play a few bars on the little pump organ. In a small sitting room facing the courtyard garden, we visited awhile. She told me more about her family, the sacrifices along the way, and confessed some regrets. Going off to finish lunch preparations, she sent me to the living room to look around. There were flowers everywhere, both inside and out, befitting this splashy, spunky lady.

Lunch was served in a tiny dining alcove off the kitchen. The kitchen was striking in itself, a room of floor-to-ceiling red cabinets set against black and white floor tiles. Over gazpacho and salad—molded tomato aspic topped with curried shrimp, surrounded by an assortment of pickled vegetables and a watermelon preserve—Phyllis Diller shared cooking tips and thrifty kitchen shortcuts.

That first visit was just the beginning of a friendship. I think of Phyllis not as a crazy, spiky-haired performer with a trademark cackle but as a hard-working and courageous woman who dared to develop her talents against extraordinary odds. That she continued to take an interest in Bluffton and in Bluffton's first woman president still surprises me as I sort through her letters and cards: "You're doing a grand job," she wrote by way of encouragement. Her Christmas cards always brought a smile: "The Wise Men brought frankincense and myrrh. Three Wise Women would have asked directions, arrived in time to help with the birth, cleaned the stable, fixed a delicious casserole and brought practical gifts." (Christmas 2003). She reminded me, when I told her that I was returning to Virginia for retirement, that her father was born in the Shenandoah Valley.

✛

Alligator Alley

Do presidents and deans and teachers admit that they keep files of letters from students and parents, from whoever happens to write a particularly happy tribute or perhaps an unusually pointed criticism? Why do we keep them? Perhaps to reassure ourselves that our immodest hopes and fervent beliefs are not in vain, that what we do matters? And to keep us humble.

I cannot bring myself to give up a bulging packet of notes and letters filed as "kudos for encouragement." Nor can I resist occasionally perusing the folder of correspondence labeled "the crazy and strange." In a series of letters addressed to me by name, a correspondent outlines plans to make some fifty persons millionaires, and Bluffton is on that list. That news is enough to get any president excited. But there is more. This is the individual who reveals that God has asked him to usher in the end of the world. "I started on the task," he writes, and "am way behind schedule." He also assures me that he has been checked repeatedly by every known means and pronounced mentally sound, even in a revelation by God, Himself.

A president gets a fair share of letters of appreciation. It is quite wonderful to pass on to a professor the accolades sent by a parent or student, letting me know that our lofty educational goals do translate into reality. These more than make up for the occasional parent tirade about a son or daughter's undeserved parking ticket or the lack of playing time their student athlete is given on the basketball floor.

While some letters are quirky and strange, they are invariably interesting. "Just a short note to let you know how I feel.

I'm back of you 100%. Sometimes a school like ours has a little trouble with the opposition. It takes a lot of united prayer to fight the enemy. . . . I just want you to know I am praying for you." I smile when I read this, wondering about the "opposition" and the "enemy," but grateful for the prayers of this friend.

I love the mystery of some of these letters, such as the one that arrived with only one word, centered, on a folded blank sheet of paper:

"R e s t i t u t i o n."

The envelope was marked "PERSONAL" and enclosed with the letter was $200. Another time an individual sent in a check for $100, explaining that he had had a couple of "life-changing experiences" and wanted to apologize for eating food from the cafeteria, received with the assistance of an accomplice, for which he had not paid.

And then there are the letters from those worried about the theological soundness of the school. Mrs. E writes from Wisconsin: "How do you view the story of Jonah in the Old Testament? Is abortion and homosexuality sinful?" I was reminded of one of my predecessor presidents. When Dr. Lloyd Ramseyer was asked whether he believed in the biblical account of Jonah and the whale, so the story goes, he responded, "Yes, I believe the whale swallowed Jonah. And if the Bible had said that Jonah swallowed the whale, I would believe that too."

Mrs. E's test question about my beliefs came just at the time I was scheduled to visit donors and alumni in Florida. It was March already. Winter would soon give way to spring. Amid getting ready for the trip, packing my bags and trying to clear the desk, I was juggling preparations for a half-dozen upcoming assignments—a sermon in Illinois, a mother-daughter dinner in Indiana, an Ohio Association of Women in Education panel. My assistant and I laughed with some disbelief when we discovered in a printed piece that I would be making a Kiwanis appearance somewhere—this was news to both of us. On one level, I knew already that I loved the work. But during those early months, I felt also a piercing sense of inadequacy. "I'm not sure I want to do this," I find scribbled in a journal entry in early spring of that first year in the presidency.

The timing of the Florida trip was fortuitous—a much needed "time out" six months into the job. It was on an extended flight to Tallahassee via Dayton and Atlanta that I finally had space to read and reflect. I had stuck in my briefcase a new book I was eager to scan. *Common Fire* was timely, as evidenced by my reading notes:

> . . . about listening to our inner voices; important to avoid burnout; discerning the links between the momentous and the minor; to keep sorting the important from the trivial; confession—forgiveness; on vision; "stopping in a world gone busy"; the reminder of friend Karen's question, "Are you preserving your Saturday mornings?"

It was on the long Saturday drive through Alligator Alley on Florida's Route 75, the connector between the west side of the state and the Atlantic coast, that I became conscious of an inexplicable peace. Traveling from Naples to Fort Lauderdale across desolate stretches of the Everglades, at first I was able to see little except pathetic swamp growth and stunted tree stands. About halfway across that strange territory, the scene changed. Or maybe it was I who was gaining second sight? Entering the Miccosukee Indian Reservation, the horizon expanded. The highway was bordered on each side by alligator canals and, here and there, a lone fisherman.

Marble black egrets perched on the bushes and small trees, with an occasional pure white egret breaking the pattern. The scene was breathtakingly beautiful as flocks of birds swooped and circled across the vast swamp. In that lonely stretch, the frenzied and tilting world settled back into quiet and slowness.

✝

The Vision Thing

Finishing *Common Fire* on the trip south yielded new insights as I continued to find my way in an unfamiliar leadership role. One of these dealt with the "vision thing." I had always admired leaders who were able to articulate a clear vision of where they were headed and how to get there. At a much earlier point in my administrative career, I had struggled with the question of what was my "vision," assuming, somehow, that every dean or president ought to have a serviceable vision, some grandiose plan, to whip out on cue. The truth was, I did not possess such a vision, at least not one I would have judged worthy the label. I felt this lack personally, afraid I was missing something in the core of my being.

These vague fears coalesced one May morning walking alone on a cold beach on the Pacific. The year was 1985. I had returned to Oregon to defend my dissertation, having completed nearly one year as academic dean in Virginia. I was feeling the weight of administrative responsibilities and expectations that I would be able to articulate a grand scheme for the future if I were to continue an academic leadership role.

Even while begging God for a vision—with none forthcoming—I sensed with faint assurance that the vision ("whatever that is," I told myself at the time) would be given, shaped or discovered, not by me alone but through my work with colleagues. I began to see that one of my responsibilities was to enable others to be what they could be. Once again I was confronting my perceived deficiencies, not at all understanding the new sense of confidence, optimism, and energy I felt as I left

the screeching seagulls, stepped around the ropes of oily sea-
weed, and headed back from the shore.

If this call to leadership was God's doing, then God would
have to help me figure it out. It was a small comfort later to hear
a distinguished college leader, J. Lawrence Burkholder, say that
a president's vision "should be the synthetic dream of many aspirations of a people representing a slice of history," as I noted
in my journal early in the Bluffton presidency. I kept listening—and reading. I noted the report of the *Common Fire* researchers who concluded that few of the "visionaries" they
interviewed could describe a clear vision of the future. This was
such reassurance to a novice president that I jotted down their
findings:

> We came to realize that while most do have a powerful
> sense of purpose, and often personal vision, they are not
> visionaries in the usual sense: people who conjure a com-
> pelling image of the future, articulate the goal, and then
> invite others to follow them. Rather than spell out an ex-
> plicit vision, or attempt to impose one on others, they
> instead described a more participatory stance, preferring
> to establish conditions for shared envisioning, staying
> closer to shifting circumstances and "proceeding as the
> way opens." They seemed more responsive, in short, to
> the context.

My friend Anne, an Ohio colleague president, concluded
that vision is less important than igniting passion—that our job
is to channel the vision of others. I was learning that my lofty
concepts of "vision" needed re-vision; that vision could be discovered and find expression in the manners and practices of a
style of servant leadership. At times of self-doubt, I sometimes
returned to Henri Nouwen: "Yes, we must dare to opt consciously for our chosenness and not allow our emotions, feelings or passions to seduce us into self-rejection." If I felt a
certain inability to create on my own an assured, inspiring vision, I would not forget that I had been called to this work.

The hype about vision remained, however, particularly in business and academic circles where the fads of leadership and management theories came and went. Strategic planning and the pursuit of excellence, concepts too often degenerating into clichés, were often framed in terms of an assumed vision.

One Sunday morning, with a respectable number of years in the presidency behind me, the congregational hymn selection was the familiar, "Be Thou my Vision"—a hymn I did not actually like very much. While the voices around me rose and fell, I remembered the surf pounding the sand that day on the Pacific when vision seemed far away. I had made peace, despite the anguish, with my own insufficiencies. Actually, I had come to embrace a concept of vision which was not about me but about eliciting the faith, hope, and dreams of the community for a purposeful future. With experience and the deep satisfaction of ten years in the presidency, I realized anew it never had been about my vision or lack thereof.

✛

Only the Wisdom of Humility

I pull off the shelf a dog-eared paperback, T. S. Eliot's *Four Quartets,* and am reminded that experience can teach us only so much compared to "the wisdom of humility ("East Coker").

The seasons of the presidency were shaped by experience, certainly, but also by a growing conviction that only the naïve and foolish delude themselves into believing the leader is ever in control. Perhaps experience is overrated. Good sense, discriminating judgment, a healthy sense of humor, a down-to-earth sensibility, and a spirit of gratitude are essential qualities of an effective leader.

As the first three or four years in office evolved into the second stage of the presidency, I kept a running list of thoughts on leadership—advice to myself. This list, which changed frequently, served as a reminder of the essence of the work as I attempted to sort out what I was learning. I simply had to write it down, as though through words I could grasp the irrational, the capricious, and the unpredictable. Here is a sampling:

Thoughts on Leadership . . .
for Encouragement, Humility, Survival

- Being able to rest in uncertainty is almost impossible but necessary.
- To be effective, leaders must live in a world not of "either/or" but rather of "both/and."
- The nature of the job: it has been observed that leaders experience higher high's and lower lows than others—those highs and lows also come closer together.

- The two best prayers I know, "Help me, help, me, help me." And "Thank you, thank you, thank you" (with credit to Anne Lamott). And sometimes the only prayer is, "God have mercy."
- Pay attention to the nudges, one of God's favorite ways of working.
- One of the wonders of the journey is being surprised by joy. But, a caution—look out when something good happens.
- Life is messy; organizations are incredibly messy. Messy is good.
- There is no shame in leaving some things to God.
- Risk is a given. But there may also be a time for sheer recklessness.
- Leaders must be clear-eyed about betrayals, failures, self-lessness, and magnanimity in human relationships.
- "Be shrewd as serpents and innocent as doves"—it's politics.
- The challenge is not to yield to seductive polarities; the middle way is an honored one.
- Be thankful—especially when in some rare quietness a creative idea erupts with astonishing possibilities.
- Leaders must inspire remembering and expectation—the two ingredients of hope.

I was finding also that leadership is mostly evidenced in the day-to-day demands of the job—listening, encouraging, discerning, serving, nurturing community, and modeling collaboration. And yes, by just showing up—at funerals, sports events, freshmen orientation, student recitals and senior art exhibitions, Homecoming, memorial dedications, the Chamber of Commerce Christmas dinner, the village library dedication, the launch of a campaign, state association meetings, artist receptions, weekly chapel, faculty forum, the Nativity candlelight service, or the birthday party of a 100 year-old alumna.

The ordinary—and mostly joyous—obligations of the office required a continual readiness to offer words of welcome to parents, students, trustees, alumni, campus visitors, churchmen, community leaders, education notables, and, once in awhile, celebrities. There were expectations of formal presidential words to be served up on demand at special conferences, education seminars, book readings, author recognitions, ground breakings, and building dedications. I was called on to offer more than my share of public prayers, both on and off campus. Sometimes I wished I had even a sliver of the eloquence and wit of the seventeenth-century "occasional poets" renowned for their ability to render an event memorable simply by a turn of phrase.

However, I did have an extensive library that I often turned to when I needed inspiration for these multi-occasions. My seemingly impractical choice of a degree in English literature turned out despite myself to be the best preparation that I could have had for the college presidency. I continued to read widely and often drew on clipping files bulging with stories and commentary on everything from the ancients to contemporary affairs. I frequently returned also to the writings of the founders of the university, whose initial vision and purpose inspired me personally and continued to guide the institution one hundred years later. Their texts and subtexts served me well as I sought to represent the ideals and principles which gave substance to the work of the education community.

Many of the president's duties were great fun—donning aprons with the vice presidents to carve and serve turkey at the student Thanksgiving feast, serving midnight breakfast during exam week, judging all sorts of contests, hosting the international students in our home, and welcoming carolers at Christmas.

On occasion, I said "no" as I did just a few weeks after I had arrived on campus. I chose not to don a toga and participate in the new student "Olympic Games" at orientation as had been the practice of the previous president. The student planners who showed up in my office that first fall to invite me were in a dilemma. What would they do with this first woman president?

Should I be included in the toga race or would they risk offend-ing me if they did not invite me? In their imaginations, they were no doubt calling up the comparison of my small, non-ath-letic frame with that of the president who had just preceded me—a distinguished six-foot, silver-haired gentleman. The stu-dents gathered in my office that day had to have been enor-mously relieved when I declined the toga race.

The supportive wife role had been a given in the school's tradition with regard to the president and his spouse's activities. So the campus adjustments to a woman president affected my husband as well. We were greatly amused when we discovered that the president's spouse was to serve ex officio on the Women's Council, an auxiliary group that organized fund-rais-ing projects for student scholarships and for academic needs. This was not the first time that Del had been in such a position, and he derived a particular satisfaction in hosting these women for an annual breakfast at our house and making himself useful in their projects.

There were times in the normal course of the days, weeks, months, and cycles of the academic year when both Del and I were on the verge of exhaustion, simply because of the pace of activities. While I did not have a "wife," I had a wonderfully supportive husband who did more than his share at home and who was unfailingly *there* when I needed him. Over the double bathroom sinks in the morning, we would review the prospects of the day or pick up a strand of unfinished business that needed attending to.

But it was the long walks around the village that helped us relax amid near impossible schedules. We had our favorite routes, heading down Spring Street and on through the Buck-eye Park, crossing Main and then circling the quarry. Some-times we hiked through campus or walked the length of Main Street, lined with stately Victorian homes. We took in the splendor of sunsets out behind the football field, and some-times we stopped to pick up a few glossy buckeyes along Bent-ley Road. We watched for the great blue heron that occasionally made an appearance along the creek. These excursions were for exercise, we told ourselves, but in fact they were much more. We kept up a brisk pace as we took up any number of mundane and strategic issues. Running a college is not brain surgery, as someone has observed, but it has its own unique challenges. When I tended to rant about a particular encounter or unexpected development, Del was there to remind me of the big picture and to help me see past my petty irritations and disappointments.

✠

Chopping Onions

If a vigorous walk around the town helped put things in perspective, equally therapeutic were the simple pleasures of returning to the kitchen. It was during a critical decision time regarding the new Academic Center that resting in uncertainty seemed best expressed by going home and cooking a meal.

On this Saturday morning, alone in the office, I was preparing for an upcoming meeting with key trustees. Money for the center's construction was trickling in and a decision had to be made about proceeding. This was the morning I received an e-mail from a professor who years before had had to be released. The note was unexpectedly affirming, which I did not deserve, I felt, given my part in the decision. I remembered another surprise, remarks a few days before at an athletic awards dinner. A team captain and basketball star expressed appreciation for the president "who worked her butt off to get us into the HCAC [athletic conference]." *That's as good as it gets*, I thought.

But there was still the funding challenge as I concluded my work that Saturday morning in the office. I decided to set the worries aside, and I headed home to prepare for guests. It was to be a simple meal, *Pakistani Kima*. I knew that whatever the pressing challenge of the moment, a few hours in the kitchen would be time well spent. I noted in my journal: "The rice is cooked, the sheets are in the laundry. Now I will chop the onions and the tomatoes, make the salad dressing and the lemon dessert. Set the table . . . thanking God for health and the joy of hospitality, the enjoyment of the smells and tastes and textures" (March 21, 1998).

Cooking did not always help, however. Often I simply had to acknowledge my own inadequacies for the task and return to the promises of Scripture: "Now what I am commanding you today is not too difficult for you or beyond your reach. . . . No, the word is very near you; it is in your mouth and in your heart" (Deut. 30:11, 14). There were mornings, when I arrived in the office surveying the demands of the day, that I literally pulled down off the shelf my bulky brown New International Version and traced out the Deuteronomy passage with my index finger. I needed to feel the smoothness of the page, to touch the words: "Now what I am commanding you today is not too difficult for you or beyond your reach." Those words and the conviction that the task I had been given was a part of some larger plan gave me strength. Opting for chosenness seems scandalous, to be sure, but alongside the surprises of my own unfolding path, other poets, prophets and priests gave me much to ponder. It was as though the words of Henri J. M. Nouwen in *Life of the Beloved* were reading me:

> [W]hen we realize that God has chosen us from all eternity, sent us into the world as the blessed ones . . . can't we, then, also trust that our little lives will multiply themselves and be able to fulfill the needs of countless people? This might sound pompous and self-aggrandizing, but, in truth, the trust in one's fruitfulness emerges from a humble spirit.

✛

Keep Me from Stupid Sins

Ten years in the presidency is a long time. The average tenure of a college president is just under seven years, those keeping track of such things tell us. Ten years is a sufficient span of time to have absorbed any number of lessons, though I confess that some of those lessons are never learned completely. It is not as though one could master Leadership 101 by the end of three or four years and then receive a certification of competence for the next stage.

As a farm girl who had never aspired to such a position, I suppose I should acknowledge that I did grow in self-confidence, in my ability to fill the public role. That was the question pressed on me by a member of the presidential search committee: Could I fill the role? I knew it was not an obvious question, hearing overtones of something unstated. But at the same time I was not sure what the interrogator was really asking. Was it a reference to being the first woman president of the college? To my stature—barely five feet? To my candor in admitting that I was not sure that I was up to the job?

Experience eventually brought me a clearer sense of what filling the office meant. It required a willingness to forego to a great extent the privilege of privacy. It meant balancing a naturally practical, down-to-earth approach with the necessity of a certain amount of pomp and ceremony. Filling the role meant speaking for others, entering with enthusiasm into a set of sometimes elusive leadership patterns. Filling the role required dancing around the minefields of campus, constituency, and community politics and not yielding to hypocrisy or cynicism.

Then there was the not infrequent in-breaking of joy and surprise—this too was a part of the work.

In a certain sense, I considered myself an accidental president—being in the right place at the right time. Flitting around the question of filling the role was the old tension between hubris and humility. Pride was a sin, I had been taught. But filling the role required boldness of action, confidence in direction, expressing personal and corporate pride in notable achievements, judging right and wrong, and striving for exceptional performance.

Humility required, on the other hand, a recognition that one's judgments needed to be tested and shaped by community and a spirit of collaboration; and that the pursuit of truth—of right action—was not a single or solitary path. The opposite of humility is not pride, I came to understand, but unmitigated arrogance in the sureness of one's position.

Because I believed so passionately in the transformative possibilities of education, it was easy to be the spokesperson for the university. Easy, once I got used to being a public person. I was inspired by the students I learned to know, by their ideals and dedication to making the world a better place. Likewise, I was humbled to be part of a community that dedicated itself to learning—to seeking truth—that sought to bring together aspirations of the heart and the mind. Every once in a while I was taken aback by the sheer symbolic power of the president's position and its sometimes hilarious expressions. There is a strand of comic absurdity in being invited (and expected) to head a village parade, riding in a powder blue vintage Cadillac convertible like some kind of celebrity.

I never did master the queenly, restrained hand wave, but I got pretty good at throwing candy to the waiting children. I managed to look as dignified as possible under the circumstances as I caught glimpses along the parade route of village friends and town officials. The whole thing seemed so ridiculously distant from the plain, simple virtues of life in a Mennonite rural community that I still grin when I think about it.

On the other hand, there were unexpectedly sweet revelations about the symbolism inherent in the position of a college president. One day one of the seniors came asking a favor. Kevin, a pre-engineering student, was large and loomed over most of his friends. Looking down at me, he confessed that he and a group of friends wished that just once they could eat lunch in the "Presidents Room."

This private room off the hallway to the student dining room was a frequent meeting place for committees convened by the president or vice presidents. The Presidents Room was also available by request to professors for luncheons with prospective faculty or for special work groups. Students would observe the comings and goings of the Trustee Executive Committee on occasion and of the President's Cabinet gathering round the teakwood conference table for bi-weekly sessions. They would observe the dining staff delivering early breakfasts and pots of coffee, or sometimes glimpse the accoutrements of this private space when the clean-up crew left the door ajar after a dinner for a special guest.

"Of course," I said to Kevin. The Presidents Room was for me a workroom, a convenient center-of-campus gathering place. But I was not unaware of the mystique surrounding the comings and goings of decision-makers who used the room and of the allure of the trappings of power. Then Kevin invited me to join the fellows for lunch. That was the ultimate compliment.

There are moments when one can only say, "This is it. This is why I am a college president." It was late September. The wooded campus was luminous with light and color. There was a gathering in the library of faculty, a few staff and a number of retirees from the community. They were there to hear Dr. Perry Bush talk about his writing project. Describing his research for the publication of a one-hundred-year history of Bluffton, Professor Bush disclosed the satisfactions and struggles of the project and introduced tantalizing snippets of scandal and stories of courage discovered in the research.

Enthralled by the professor's revelations and drawn in by his animated presentation, the audience sat captivated by what they were hearing. I kept watching the faces of the old-timers: the retired and much-loved Latin teacher, the harpsichord craftsman and music lover and his wife, and the widow of a former distinguished biology professor. In my line of sight, as I listened to the presentation, were the newcomers to campus—the new religion teacher and other recently appointed faculty sitting there with students who had come to hear their favorite professor. That day, in the magnificent Georgian reading room looking out through the high arched windows at the fall foliage, I thought to myself, *This is why I am a college president.*

It was an ineffable moment, having something to do with a community of scholars, the passion for the college's mission, and respect for the founders. That gathering embodied a commitment to pass on knowledge to the next generation; it revealed the camaraderie of folks who had struggled in the early years, who survived and were now being honored by their story being told. That moment of revelation no doubt had something to do also with the palpable beauty of the old library tables and the heavy oak chairs, the display of books authored by faculty—all contributing to a singular event offering glimpses of community shaped by deep streams of faith and enlivened by a spirit of inquiry.

Through ten years in the presidency I gained an increasing appreciation for institutions, for their immense possibilities despite failures and bumbling complexities. I was often confronted with both the fragility of the human actors in our organizations and communities and also with their strength and perseverance in the face of immeasurable loss—the death of a student, a moral lapse, acknowledging the end of a dream, accepting failure, or confronting betrayal. I learned that there is virtually nothing more exhilarating than working with a leadership team that evidences a synergy and creativity born of a common purpose. This included the President's Cabinet, as we called the administrative team that gave leadership to the areas of academic program, student services, finances, religious life, and fund raising; and it included an unusually congenial and visionary board of trustees. Working with stellar leaders was my great good fortune as a college president.

When I was subjected to the occasional bragging of fellow university presidents about their successes, I felt the old upsurge of doubt and wondered about my own suitability for the job. But for the most part, there were enough challenges and rewards to keep me focused on my own campus and energized by the stream of growth and creative programs which marked the late 1990s and early years of the new century.

Coming to the conclusion of my presidency, I found myself returning to the same overriding themes of the first years: an enormous sense of gratitude and, simultaneously, a keen understanding that experience does not mean the job gets easier or the path becomes clearer. There is a certain freedom of spirit that grows out of the realization that our work is larger than any one person; that the work is not in fact our work, but God's. I found myself returning again and again in my early morning reading to those sages and saints who saw life whole and who were not discouraged by the reality of limits and the untidiness of organizations and the human situation.

Some of this wisdom came directly from Scripture. I was taken by a modern version of one of the Psalm prayers: "Lord, keep me from stupid sins" (Ps. 19:13, *The Message*). All of us, if we are honest, acknowledge mistakes and misjudgments. The hardest to forgive are one's own "stupid sins" which are recognized only in retrospect. It is little comfort to pick up the *USA Today* and read the headline, "Even Good CEO's Pick the Wrong Direction." For me it was more instructive to share openly over the years with a small group of colleague presidents who were clear-eyed about the work and who shared vulnerabilities and fears with one another. I was also a student of those leaders who saw themselves as servants rather than heroes. They reassured me by their questions and willingness to acknowledge uncertainty that leadership does not mean knowing it all.

At each stage of the presidency—initiation into a new challenge and into a brand new setting, then becoming inspired by and comfortable with the day-to-day work of the office, and finally bringing to completion those goals which had been established through dreaming, debate, discussion, and deliberative action—I learned new lessons. These were all informed by a paradoxical sense of peace amid anxiety, of an unassailable joy amid occasional despair, and a measure of confidence even when the future was murky. I often returned to Flannery O'-Connor's advice, knowing exactly what she meant: "Be properly scared and go on doing what you have to do."

I remembered my grandson Tyler who, as a two-year-old at a family beach outing, was frightened of the waves. And then, getting his feet wet and guided by his dad or granddad, declaring, "I'm not afraid," as he emerged from the ocean dripping wet. That is as good a description of the presidency as any I can think of, recognizing that there is always another crashing wave rolling in just when circumstances seem relatively calm and secure.

I experienced the seasons of the presidency as more cyclical than progressive, as life-giving while at the same time utterly exhausting, as redeemed by in-breaking evidences of grace through personnel crises and student tragedies. I learned amid nagging anxieties to yield to the energizing power of those dark times which thrust me totally into the steam of God's mercy. Altogether, the ten years at Bluffton confirmed for me that God's inscrutable ways can scarcely be imagined, let alone predicted. I still find the Psalmist prayer one for all seasons: "Keep me from stupid sins, from thinking I can take over your work."

PART SIX

LIFE WORK

✠

For Love of the Work

There is work and then there is Work. All the repetitive chores at home, the cleaning, cooking, and laundry, were clearly work. Even the summer jobs to earn a little money—enduring sunburn and a sore back from the bean and strawberry fields or hiring out as a domestic (because Mennonite girls knew how to work)—were unquestionably hard labor. The focus was on getting it over with, on managing to stave off tedium or tiredness or boredom, and on earning a few dollars.

But work with a capital W was something else, some mysterious beckoning to come thither, to try new things, to test know-how and ability, to hone skills, to experiment, and to win approval. My mother managed to combine both kinds of work in her daily homemaking routines. She demonstrated that one could love even what we called housework, and she did this quietly and with common-sense humility.

I was only gradually to learn the fullest meaning of Work, what I would call life work. I caught a glimpse of this in Wendell Berry's essay reflections on *What are People For?* With him, I would say, "Seeing the work that is to be done, who can help wanting to be the one to do it?" And then there is Donald Hall's sideways comment about work: "Contentment is work so engrossing that you do not know that you are working." Neither of these propositions, however, speaks to the ongoing journey of surprise that has been the most conspicuous feature of my own understanding of life work.

Early on as a college leader, I remember another president's statement (but not the person who said it) insisting, "I just love all those problems." At the time it seemed courageous and admirable. Now it feels at best like an overstatement to make a point or at worst just rhetoric. The general work flow of the president's office feels more like the title of a book I ran across during a particularly frenzied week: *The Extravagant Universe: Exploding Stars, Dark Energy, and the Accelerating Cosmos.* That, I told myself, is about as good a description as any for the experience of a college administrator.

I dimly recognized also, as the race car driver Mario Andretti once observed, that if you are in control, you are not going fast enough. The challenge, I discovered, was to find some order, to identify the still point amid those million (more or less) impulses firing in the brain simultaneously: impressions, dormant questions, procrastinations, unarticulated fears, overwhelming gratitude, small-minded exasperations, curiosity, bursts of delight, boldness, weak-kneed wavering, and surety. And to recognize amid it all, a certain peace.

"At least it is never boring," a colleague and I used to say to one another, acquainted on a daily basis with the vagaries and perversities of human failings. We learned to expect the unexpected and were on occasion happily confounded by revelations of selfless sacrifice and extraordinary service. Caught up in the careening trajectories of academe generally, while becalmed by the orderly cycles of the year, I intuitively understood several things: that relationships are paramount, that respectful dialogue is essential, and that one must never underestimate the complexity of community symbols and their interpretation in what appear to be straightforward actions. In the face of the nitty-gritty—a faculty petition, for example; a tenure denial; a student request to fly a POW flag; a racial flare-up centered around a confederate flag and an ill-considered prank with a noose—it sometimes seemed in relating to faculty and students that parenting skills were every bit as critical as leadership know-how.

How could a thoughtless and insensitive remark lead to such hullabaloo? I sometimes wondered. Is this director naïve or is she devious? Or there was the time I arrived at my office at

6:50 a.m. and saw the red message light blinking. I picked up. A quiet voice: "This is Max Miller at 168 Latimer Avenue. It's about 12:40 a.m. There is a disturbance at the college and I am going to call the police." That was it. There was no subsequent call to indicate the outcome. Thankfully, Mr. Miller had not phoned me at home in the middle of the night.

Then there was the call one morning when it was barely light. Del, who was already up, picked up the phone. I hauled myself out of bed, hearing him say "band camp," bringing back the horrors of the scaffolding accident at a previous summer program. This caller was a village resident complaining about being disturbed by the loud band music coming from campus. She was so irate that she gave Del a piece of her mind: "This is not the way to be a good neighbor."

The caller was right. It was too early for anyone to be awakened by trumpets, clarinets, tubas, and drums. I made a quick call. The summer programs director agreed to go to campus immediately and set things right. This was the day before Bluffton would officially become a university, and it was important, we all understood, to keep working at village relations.

How to remain above the fray but continue wisely engaged was often the challenge. By nature my inclination was to smooth over, to soften, and to encourage rather than to provoke; but that did not mean I was spared the need to confront difficult and unreasonable personalities and at times to make unpopular decisions. During a particularly messy time, I took such comfort in the words of Kathleen Norris that I jotted down in my journal her conviction that

> being God's chosen does not mean doing well. It does not grant access to all the answers but means contending with hard questions, thankless tasks, and usually a harrowing journey . . . [Christ chooses] to employ our weaknesses rather than our strengths, and our failures far more than our successes. (*Amazing Grace*)

Intuitively I knew, despite whatever commotion was stir-

ring at the moment, that it was ultimately about being called to
the work; it was about loving the work. It was about entering
into something that was much larger and deeper than any singular vocational choice. I also recognized that the occasional
longing for a less stressful life was not a true desire but a fugitive
temptation. It usually disappeared if I ignored it. In fact, I understood at some unexamined level that too much comfort was
deadly and that chaos, conflict, jolts, and unsettling perplexities
were necessary to maintain an edge of creativity.

Sometimes I wrote things down, making notes in my journal, just to see if I could slow the spinning, tilted, pell-mell
world just a little. It was a way also to savor the fullness of the
work and to acknowledge a certain contradiction: a longing for
peace and quiet while at the same time drawing life and energy
from the vitality of the people I met and the folks I worked
with.

Developing the synergies of a superb leadership team also
was essential to keep everything in perspective. Together we
worked at managing the tensions between restraint and im-
petuousness, risk and security, tradition and change. In the
rambunctiousness of it all, we debated, reasoned, and made decisions; on occasion we simply took a leap in the dark, recognizing that not all actions should be purely rational. As one of the
vice presidents asked one day, "Where's faith in all of this?"

I was often aware in even the most routine encounters that
each day was sacred in its own way. This might be in crossing
paths with the student emptying the trash cans in College Hall
or checking in with the staff next door who were moving into
newly renovated space.

I remember the small things: the warm greeting from
Coach driving past me in the evening as I walk home; the
chance meeting of a college alumna at the produce stand behind the Dairy Freeze where we stop and visit. Mike in dining
services never fails to smile when I see him, and I exchange a few
pleasantries in the restroom with Amy, a student who considers
me her friend because I put in a good word for her when she felt

she had been unfairly treated. I sort through salary contracts, and I send out notes to the stream of well-wishers who went out of their way to congratulate Bluffton on its university status. These are the outward evidences of the commitments that bring a community together.

In greeting those I meet as I head for an appointment in Centennial Hall or in the student center, I find myself wondering: What fears, hopes, and burdens energize and constrain these wonderful members of this education community? I am aware again that it is the ordinary, daily encounters that most often reveal that which is irreplaceable, worthy of awe, and beyond human understanding. Work is often about the unremarkable "stuff."

✠

Conversation at the Bathroom Sink

Work, good work, is a subject of endless fascination to me. It is in our work that we experience the possibilities of transformation. Getting ready in the morning at the double bathroom sinks, Del and I occasionally have bits and pieces of conversation about work. Most of this is just the ordinary checking in with one another: "What is your day like today?" Or, "Will you be home for supper?" These questions might come from either of us. But somewhere around the twenty-fifth year of our marriage, it dawned on me that Del and I viewed work in very different ways.

I used to be both amused and exasperated at him for looking forward to retirement, this well before we could have been called middle-aged. (We used to argue about that too. Just when did one become middle-aged?) I did not want to think about retirement; I had just undertaken a new position as academic dean. Sometimes long walks gave us time to explore our very different attitudes about our jobs. We still pick up threads of this conversation now and then, and I hope it does not end soon. I am not sure that we have it figured out yet.

What I do know is that for my husband work was something you did because you had to and got it out of the way as quickly as possible. It was God's curse on humankind for yielding to temptation, for eating the forbidden fruit. Growing up on a homestead in Idaho, Del sometimes had had to miss school to help with farm work. He learned from his father to work single-mindedly, immersing himself fully in whatever job he undertook. He was taught the virtue of hard work. By dint of sheer personal effort, it seemed, one might redeem the curse.

We were both shaped by community values of work as close to godliness. And we were brought up to understand that women and men had very different roles to play in the world of work. A husband was the head of the household and needed to support his family. The women were primarily responsible to rear the children and to do whatever needed to be done.

I had no career goals. I did not consider my future in terms of choosing a life work. Actually, vocational goals for women would have been suspect in my church community. I just knew that I wanted an education and would worry about the rest later.

Eventually, when I was offered a "real job" in an academic office, I discovered what I would have had no way of knowing at all, that I loved the work: advising students, managing the office, listening to faculty concerns, organizing summer school, implementing new program initiatives, and working with the budget. It was a job, I sometimes thought, that I would have paid to do. My experience was one of liberation; I was involved firsthand with exciting initiatives, problem solving, working with people of marvelous talent; I was constantly being challenged to tackle new things.

There is something about life that is grossly unfair when one spouse feels shackled by the necessity of work through circumstance and family conditioning and the other thrives in the freedom that comes with work. Much of this grows out of a particular time, the late 1960s and early 1970s, when the women's liberation movement was having a significant impact. Even my own daughters will never fully understand why I felt so fortunate in the opportunities which came my way as I went from administrative assistant to assistant to the dean to assistant dean to vice-president for academic affairs and then eventually to president. I was granted a particular privilege—the privilege of choice—while, as my husband would remind me, men had to work to be respectable, to fulfill societal expectations.

That Del and I were each other's best friend helped us to laugh about our differing views where work was concerned. He fully supported me in my peculiar exuberances, while I mostly humored him in his occasional fantasies about retirement; and we continued to make peace with our philosophical differences. My sense of contentment lay in the work itself. His would be most fully realized when the job was no longer an externally imposed burden.

In our particular religious tradition, Adam and Eve's disobedience and the curse of sin was emphasized in the biblical story. In the Genesis account, God condemns Adam and Eve to daily lives of pain and suffering when they are driven out of the Garden of Eden. What is too often obscured in our rendering of the salvation narrative is the holiness of work as demonstrated by a God who brings into existence the cosmos and humankind. I concluded that experiencing delight and satisfaction in one's work is a godly thing. Who can argue with Genesis 1 where God pronounces the creation *good* and then rests from the work?

Work and rest, creation and reflection, doing and being are all part of what it means to be human. Whatever tangents Del and I might mull over in our continuing conversations about work, we both consider work as calling. For us, calling has been a partnership on a journey of the unexpected. An underlying sense of wonder and astonishment at life grows out of this particular sense of calling as we become aware of the currents of mystery which shape our lives.

✛

"Tell Me Your Plans"

I love the Midrash saying, "Tell God your plans and listen to him laugh." My version of that would be, "God tell me your plans and listen to me laugh." The unfolding of my particular life's work has grown mostly out of convergences of the unexpected. I have never been prepared quite for what others thought I could do. And then I would be just foolish enough to take a risk and see if they were right. I find myself teetering on some invisible line balanced between absurdity and awe.

I recall the first and only time I went skiing on Mt. Hood. I was in my early twenties. A group of Portland youth serving in VS (Mennonite Voluntary Service) had decided on a lark to take the day off and get in some skiing. Del and I were filling in temporarily at the house as unit leaders so were invited along. I have few memories of that day except that after spending some time with the beginners and getting a feel for the basics, I was persuaded to tackle a slope that was much beyond my ability. Hovering at the top of a sharp drop-off, skis lined up appropriately, I was urged to let go and sail away.

I have thought of that moment since as a perfect emblem of a decision crossroads embodying the temptation to recklessness tempered by the terror of failure. I made a foolish decision. I pushed off down that steep slope. Fortunately, I was so inexperienced that I did not get far before plunging into the snow. That I did not crash into a tree or break a leg in the fall was God's providence, I am sure, which I surely did not deserve. Despite my saving fall on the more advanced slope, that one day's adventure was an unforgettable thrill. Although the experience never led to an overwhelming urge to take up skiing, that day still pulls me toward itself in some peculiar way. Like cradling a snow globe, every so often I take out the memory, hold it, turn it around, shake it, and ponder the lessons learned.

It was that cautionary Mt. Hood experience that I was to recall vividly some thirty-five years later when I was asked to consider a denominational leadership assignment, one which seemed way beyond my experience or ability. I was driving back late one September night from the Toledo airport, now a couple of years into the presidency at Bluffton. Returning home from a session-packed two-day conference in New England, I had a good hour's drive. This would give me a chance to catch up with Del.

Heading out Airport Road to Route 2, I picked up the car phone and dialed home. Del relayed a telephone message. The caller would try again, asking whether I would consider serving as the first moderator of the new denomination which was being formed out of two integrating churches, the Mennonite Church and the General Conference Mennonite Church. The position would involve serving also as chair of the first executive board of the two merging denominations.

The prospect made me laugh out loud. There was a certain comic absurdity to the very idea, and I said so to Del. About that time, the phone cord got caught in the stem of my glasses and I nearly drove off the road trying to disentangle myself. That seemed a good time to bring the conversation to an end. I drove the rest of the way home telling myself that I had plenty to do already and saw no reason to complicate my life. In that moment, I dismissed the question entirely.

In the days to follow, after talking with the chair of the nominating committee myself, I continued to be baffled by this strange call and wondered why I was selected. I was not a minister, and I had never held a national position in the church. As a woman educator, I was certainly not a "churchman," typically the type of person selected for such appointments. I had neither the theological nor political credentials to merit such a position.

I was encouraged to give further thought to the request, so I sought counsel from trustee confidants, colleagues, and a few persons who knew the inner workings of the church. As Del and I considered the additional responsibilities such an appointment would entail—which would affect him as well as me—and the political tensions within the denominations, I relived that sense of standing on a precipice; of hesitating at the top of the slope, ski poles in hand, wondering if I should shove off.

I was still early in the presidency at Bluffton and fully energized by innovative program initiatives, an Academic Center campaign, launching a new strategic plan and gearing up for a campus master planning process. When the denominational call came, a part of me recognized the old reckless impulse to take on a new challenge, but it was tempered by more experience. Resting there on the ledge of my mind was the matter of that "call." What did it mean? What should I do with it? For a little while, I was content to push the question around, not feeling hurried to decide. The immediacy of pressing matters gave me an excuse to procrastinate, but it was a decision which could not be put off indefinitely. Even as I sought the counsel of persons who knew me well, who knew my insufficiencies and possible contribution to a process creating a new Mennonite Church USA, I knew that reason alone would not yield an answer.

And so we walked, Del and I. On a Sunday evening we headed down Brookwood and west on Elm to enjoy the sunset over the football field. Then we turned over to Bentley Road past the dorms and the buckeye trees, past the falling leaves of the blazing trees behind College Hall and the library. Leaving the campus perimeter, we went on around the Kibler bend in the Sunday quiet, over to Main Street and more scuffing through the leaves. Sixty-six degrees the bank thermometer read, as we headed past the coffee shop, Smiths Realty, and the meat market toward the edge of the Bethel Chinese Restaurant parking lot and the entrance to the village park.

"Is it a 'call'?" one friend had asked when I had sought advice. Del and I thought about that question and about the encouragement of others in those days of indecision.

Crossing the Benroth covered footbridge at Riley Creek and then taking a path along the pond, we glimpsed a covey of mallards heading out from shore. Though it was approaching dusk, the light still reflected off the water. It was inexpressibly beautiful in the silence, and I wanted to stay. But it had to be a mere pause, a momentary breathing in of the stillness and the splendor of the ducks gliding away. It was that image, crystallizing a moment out of time, which combined grace, beauty, strength, and a sense of God's order that gave me peace about whatever decision we would make.

I was being asked again, through an unexpected telephone call, to say "yes" to work that I had not imagined doing. There was something slightly comical about these recurrent calls, it seemed to me, as though the Holy One needed to resort to modern technology. As I considered this latest proposal, being willing to accept a leadership position in launching a new denomination, I recalled those three earlier phone calls which had represented turning points in my life.

I thought back to that first call the day I was scrubbing an old carpet. It was 1974. I had just completed my Master's degree in English. I would be teaching a course or two but was ready to add an office job. The call that day from the president's office at Eastern Mennonite, where Del was now a mathematics professor, messed me up, because I had just agreed to work in the registrar's office. Now before my first day on the job I was being asked if I would switch positions and begin working in a vacancy just opened in the dean's office. That led to a mind-boggling series of opportunities over the next eight years which became a course of training in itself—schooling in higher education administration.

I also remembered that second phone call from Eastern Mennonite ten years later—1984, the year I was finishing doctoral work at the University of Oregon. During the time Del and I were on sabbatical in Oregon, the academic dean had decided to return to teaching. Would I allow my name to be considered for the job? I recalled that I initially had said "no," knowing the work and knowing that even God could not meet faculty expectations. I had not forgotten, either, that I was eventually persuaded to say "yes" simply because the faculty asked that I consider the position.

Then the third call twelve years later came to mind again. Another surprise. Would I consider a college presidency? I still have not gotten used to these telephone calls out of the blue, including the message received on the way home from the Toledo airport.

These unexpected interruptions would shake me up. They reminded me why I have always been drawn to characters in the biblical story asked to do things they felt unable to do. Especially Moses whose inability with words I found particularly comforting. Being asked to take on what at the time seemed enormous and, in some cases, near impossible challenges has been, I suppose, the literal rendering of those dreams and nightmares of heading up the mountain, of careening at breakneck speed around the curve of a disappearing highway, or of ascending Emerson's stairs which go out of sight above us. But even more disquieting and amazing was the realization that as Jesus told his disciples, "You did not choose me, but I chose you" (John 15:16).

Once the sculptor Henry Moore at age eighty was asked by a friend, "What is the secret of life?" The poet Donald Hall recounts this conversation and Moore's reply: "The secret is to devote your whole life to one ambition. . . . But remember: Choose something you can't do." And Henry Moore laughed, remembers Hall.

I am coming to understand that life work—one's vocation, calling, or whatever term one chooses—is an inevitable blending of formidable challenge, unpredictability, certitude and doubt, inexplicable contentment, turbulence, tedium, confusion, paradox, and the realization that commitment to a larger life is part of the sacred privilege and responsibility given to us by the Creator. That commitment evolved for me into a willingness to open myself to what God might be asking me to do.

My life work continues a mysterious path and includes leadership opportunities I could not have envisioned and which still puzzle me. And so I laugh along with Henry Moore in his conclusion that you must choose something that you cannot do.

Leadership: Possibilities and Limits

It was Friday, April 1, 2005. The Bluffton University board chair and I made our way to the Academic Center, where faculty and staff had gathered in Stutzman Hall. It was time to announce to the campus my decision to retire from the presidency the next year, completing ten years of service at Bluffton.

Initially I was uneasy about making this announcement more than a year before leaving, given the lame duck predictabilities of such situations within an organization. But the chair had convinced me that the search process for a new president would require time. He pressed me as to whether I was sure this was the time to complete my work at Bluffton. Del and I both had a keen sense that our decision was right, so the trustees had been informed and the chair of the board would begin to set in motion the process for identifying candidates for my successor.

Walking into the hall that Friday afternoon, I knew there had to be speculation as to what would prompt the board chair to summon the faculty and staff for a campus-wide gathering. I was met by a business professor who had been waiting for me. He eagerly handed me a brand new book, a beautiful hardback which he had gone to some pains to have the author autograph. George and I shared a common interest in organizational management and leadership theories, and we often exchanged readings.

We were drawn particularly to Margaret J. Wheatley, who approached leadership questions from a relationship perspective rather than from the old "command and control" model.

Meeting Wheatley at a conference, George had had a chance to speak with her personally.

The faculty and staff kept filing into Stutzman Hall, finding seats as the board chair and I waited at the front of the room. I thanked George, moved by this unexpected gift and his thoughtfulness. I quickly opened the book to Wheatley's autograph and these words:

> *Lee,*
> *May this book serve all us insecure ones.*
> *May we give birth to a new culture of hope.*
> *In support of your fine leadership,*
> *MWheatley 3/05*

How could she know the uncertainties, the questions I had been dealing with in the months leading up to my decision? Then George pointed out what I had failed to notice in the moment, that only part of that autograph had been written on the spot. The first two lines were pre-stamped in her cursive hand. Nevertheless, I was moved by the gesture of George's generosity and the timing of this particular gift reexamining the question of leadership. It was all about "finding our way," the title of the book; it was about resisting easy leadership formulas and embracing possibility, surprise, simplicity, and not knowing.

College presidents are always tempted by the latest leadership theories and fads. Some of us read lots of books and shamelessly borrow whatever we can to stave off our own insecurities as we strive for success and search for more effective ways to lead our institutions. We are lured by quick fixes and even by solutions to problems we did not know we had. Presidents and CEOs are intrigued by the currents which propel leaders and organizations toward greatness, however defined, and we play over and over in our minds narratives of failure and achievement, often not willing to face the fact that we are not in control; that in some ways we "make it up as we go," as Wheatley would say.

John W. Gardner made famous the saying that "the first and last task of a leader is to keep hope alive." To do that, three things are necessary I believe: to foster an appreciation for the history and tradition of a people or an organization, to cultivate a clear sense of identity in the present; and to create a sense of purpose for the future. How does one do that in the day-to-day, in the normal transactions of the work? I am convinced that celebration and remembering are key, which in turn foster a spirit of gratitude and expectation.

Each year at Bluffton's traditional New Year's dinner, faculty and staff are recognized for their service milestones: five, ten, fifteen, twenty, twenty-five, even thirty-five or forty years of service. The sum total of years celebrated in the present mount into hundreds of years, an astounding recognition of the tireless and inspired dedication of folks who work out of a sense of purpose and hope. On these occasions, colleagues write tributes, they recount stories, they remember, and they express appreciation. This community ritual is but one example of how we honor the past, celebrate the present moment, and cultivate a commitment to the future—for our students and for succeeding generations.

Even in such tedious tasks as accreditation self-studies, refining strategic plans, or creating budgets and spending plans, the possibility for imagining the future gives new life to those carrying out their work in the present. Sitting around a table in the Academic Center on a cold January day, the Council for Strategic Planning looks ahead to the August date when Bluffton will officially be recognized as a university. "What kind of university do we want to be?" we ask. We dare to lay out our best hopes, even our crazy dreams.

One of the particular privileges of a college president is engaging students as they search out a path for their own lives. This is heady work, listening to their stories, learning of their struggles, and offering a word of encouragement here and there—and sometimes advice when they asked for it. One day in early February, Sara came to see me. She had set up an appointment, this beautiful, audacious freshman from the African-American community. She had already caught my attention on two or three public occasions when she had participated in a forum discussion or stood to ask a question after the campus speaker's lecture.

Sara had a request: "Show me how to be a leader." Then, "Will you be my mentor?" I agreed and this began a relationship through which I surely learned as much as she did. We met periodically and began with practical things such as how she would establish her priorities and manage her time. Then she would report back what she was discovering, and our friendship grew.

Inevitably, it is the normal, ordinary matters that sharpen the particularity of the work we are called to do. On a rare weekend freed from travel or other obligations, it was enough to observe the pink sky as I headed out for a catch-up Saturday morning in the office; to notice the crystal snow patterns on the asphalt; to listen to the dove call in the distance. I remember a perfect morning (or as near perfect as they get, I tell myself) after a complicated and burdened week which included a concert with a Robert Frost theme, interviewing a stunning candidate for a library position, making the decision to terminate a coach's contract, and planning a campus memorial service for a student who had died tragically in a car accident. It was a week of varied encounters; some exhilarating, some profoundly painful, reminding me that we do our work with fear and trembling; that we serve out of a sense of humility, gratitude, grace and an awareness of God's faithfulness.

✦

Rumors of Power

Most days, a president does not feel very powerful, but rather at the mercy of contingencies and impositions over which she or he has little control. A truism of the academic world is that presidents have more power than they think they do but less power than the faculty believe presidents have. It is the nature of power to be suspect, an uncomfortable reality which well-meaning leaders sometimes try to ignore. In the university setting, we live in a curious tension between those ideals of shared learning and community aspirations and the necessity of structure, issuing grades, imposing limits, and relying on hierarchical decision-making.

"You are not willing to admit that you have power," a faculty member once blurted out accusingly when he was particularly exasperated with his dean—me. I winced, because I knew there was some truth in what he said. My tools were persuasion, convincing others of the desirability of one path over another, or in sorting through the evidence but being willing to let the decision go whichever way the particular group would decide. My commitment was to collaboration, working with integrity and openness, though such ideals were always hemmed in by the necessities of professional confidentiality and putting the institution's well-being ahead of individual interests.

I am convinced by Linda Hill of the Harvard Business School that an effective leader must have a mindset that includes three central beliefs: " (1) that the institution is more important than any single individual, including himself or herself; (2) the leader's job is to help others succeed; and (3) first and foremost in making decisions, the organization's future and sustainability must be considered." Those principles seem so straightforward and reasonable. Working those out in daily decisions becomes more complicated, however.

"It's hard to say 'no' to the president," one of my esteemed faculty colleagues said one day, sitting in my office when asked if he would consider a particular assignment. That forthright response took me aback. But it also reminded me again that, much as I resisted the presumption of power and authority, I had to accept the fact that my responsibility as a university president, dean, or church leader required that I exercise power.

In the case of the latter, serving as denominational executive board chair for two years, I was only mildly amused by the cheerful, supportive jokes at my expense about being the pope of the Mennonite church. Such comments simply underscored old stereotypes about power and control. They also evoked a recurring sense of incredulity and even hilarity about those convergences which had brought about unforeseen leadership opportunities.

I have become increasingly persuaded, as one of my faculty colleagues says, that the job of a leader is to listen, learn, respect, and support. For leaders to be successful, they must understand power as relational, not hierarchical. Such a model of leadership, although requiring unpopular decisions at times, overturns the old notion that the leader is responsible to control everyone and everything. The notion of relational power, of power as energy and delegated authority, I can live with.

The model of listening, learning, supporting, and respecting represents a multi-dimensional approach to leadership which requires a healthy respect for the needs of individuals as well as for the imbalances and fluctuations in an organization. I am still learning that being able to "let go" is perhaps one of the most difficult requirements of leadership, but it is sometimes the only way that moving ahead is possible. When a leader is able to trust the unfolding process and to offer a steady balance of confidence and vulnerability, then members of the organization can move out from entrenched positions and embrace change.

This matter of confidence, described by Rosabeth Moss Kanter as a "sweet spot between arrogance and despair," is not one to be taken lightly. It is important to recognize that what we are talking about is not self-confidence so much as confidence in other people. This is a view that emphasizes leadership as a constellation, not a star; leadership as plural, not singular.

Leaders who work within the sphere of Christian organizations are particularly susceptible to narrow and sometimes intractable expectations of those who have their own definition of what is "Christian." "How can a Christian university do this?" (with the emphasis on *do*), I was asked when an employee was required to give up his job. The outside critic, who was a friend of the employee, came in to see me, condemning the university out of hand for such unchristian action even though the employee was offered an alternative position.

It may be useful to recognize that institutions in themselves are not Christian, but people are. That requires that Christian leaders model for their organizations an ability to carry out and communicate with respect even those very difficult decisions that significantly affect others. It is greatly humbling to recognize that persons of authority do exercise a power for good or ill to change other people's lives. That too is a part of the responsibility of the leader.

Leadership, for all its trappings about imagining and enlivening the future, requires an ability to settle down and get the job done. It requires attention to the moment, sorting through the guff. Leadership is about stewardship, about the prudent use of resources. It is about exercising responsibility in a cluttered present. Leaders must function, as someone has said, in a "fifth dimension," at the intersection of time with the timeless. This reality is one of exploration, of moving ahead often in the dark, and of embracing possibility amid chaos. It requires living in a paradoxical state which acknowledges limits but sees also unbounded potential.

✛

Life Work: The Country of Marriage

Any personal reflections on life work would be incomplete without acknowledging the "country of marriage," that incomparable Wendell Berry description. It may be imprudent, even presumptuous, to include a spouse and one's family in a personal account, but the fact remains that there is one person with whom I have spent more time than I have with parents, siblings, or daughters. Marriage has meant an intertwined life of immeasurable bounty, but a "country" which I am wary about exploring too deeply.

Perhaps it is in the small things that one glimpses, if only for a moment, the depth and wonder of a relationship that for the most part defies definition or description. So I must fall back on vignettes. This one I call "pork roast, couscous, and cake"—shorthand for an evening Del and I were invited to dinner. The invitation was to a professor's house for conversation with colleagues and with guests from a neighboring Catholic university about organizing a joint conference around some topic of mutual interest.

Del and I both were almost too tired to imagine the evening being fun. I did not take for granted Del's uncomplaining, even gracious, assent to a whole succession of official dinners and receptions that were part of the president's job. The chance to do things together—just to *be* together—made many of these occasions bearable. We sometimes indulged in our own silly game of guessing whether we would be served chicken or beef.

However, this was a private dinner with good friends. I remember the day as "heavy," one of those lazy, throw-away terms that we latch on to when we seek to bring some reason or control to the sense that everything is falling apart. That particular day, in a succession of meetings, I noted more than usual an expectation that I was supposed to fix things. This barely disguised impulse to shift burdens to someone else is particularly endemic in academe: let someone else take care of it. In this case, they looked to me. The day began with hearing out a dissatisfied and demanding department and it concluded with a lengthy cabinet meeting. But that was not the end. When I returned to the office, most everyone else having gone home, there was a long e-mail complaint from a student that I needed to address.

Despite the grueling day, the dinner that night was wonderful: roasted garlic asparagus, fruited couscous, Greek salad, and rosemary-peppered pork loin. The dinner party was composed of persons who, as it turned out, were particularly interested in a theological conference bringing together Mennonites and Catholics. Sitting next to the guest of honor, I found my spirits considerably lifted by the charm and liveliness of Father Howard. The tiredness fell away.

We were well into the dinner. Del shifted closer and, with only a whispered word or two, asked if he might have my water since I had nearly a full glass and was already on to coffee. I nodded, and he reached for the goblet. Who could have noticed? From my other side, Father Howard leaned over to me and whispered, "That's marriage."

I was taken aback. The father did not miss a thing. But more than that, I was moved by his wonderful and profound insight. I wondered if this handsome, celibate priest terribly missed what he had given up.

Life choices, saying "yes," are inextricably bound up with one's life work. When I told my parents at age eighteen that Del and I wanted to get married, my father's probing question was, "Are you sure?" He asked it so insistently that in that moment I knew that indeed I was not sure. At the time I could not have known it, but this was to become a familiar theme: being asked to make a decision amid uncertainty; then being propelled into a choice growing out of a series of convergences and fortuities that suggested at best an unknown future.

But I was lucky (in the sacred sense), in love, in marriage, and in life work. Embarking on a partnership which was based on traditional ideals of marriage, Del and I entered happily—though perhaps without much thought—into a relationship that reflected the values of the faith community. Perhaps the only divergence was the commitment we both had to education and Del's dismissal of the whole scheme of the submissive wife and husband the head of the household. He became my greatest encourager, urging me to pay attention to the inner nudges which eventually took me down the path of higher education. We studied together and we worked together. Most days we still understand that through God's providence we have become a part of something that can be only dimly perceived.

✚

Life Work: Postscript

On June 14, 2006, I heard the announcement that Donald Hall had been named Poet Laureate of the United States. So I pulled off my shelf his book entitled *Life Work* and remembered the day ten years before when I met Donald Hall in Michigan at a conference of writers and readers. At the campus book signing, he opened my copy to the title page, asked me about myself and under *Life Work* wrote in a tiny, neat script:

for Lee
& for sanity, reading
Saturday mornings,
& work
Donald Hall
4/12/96

I am indebted to Donald Hall who over the years has inspired me not only to explore the sacred nature of work but to notice the connections between what we *do* and who we *are*—between labors of body and mind and simply resting in the heart-stopping loveliness of field and pond, of sky and earth. Jesus called attention to the lilies of the field, reminding his disciples that the normal preoccupations of work, of toil and struggle, are to be held in perspective by recognizing another pattern of being: living in the moment, trusting God, and not worrying about the future. That lesson, working itself out over a lifetime of practice, is a lesson blessed by God and a manifestation of wholeness and fullness in both one's work and being.

EPILOGUE

The Man in the Rain

On the ten-minute walk from our house at 259 Brookwood to the university, I would sometimes meet in the approaching dawn a gangly, thin man walking his dog. Usually we met as I headed up Spring Street approaching College Avenue. Sometimes the timing was off and I would glimpse him ahead crossing campus on his own private route as he disappeared through the trees. "We need umbrellas this morning," he might say as we passed one another, each trying to protect ourselves from the wind and rain. On other occasions, he would say, "A beautiful morning." "Yes it is," I would respond as we passed. Whether it was dark or beginning to turn light, it could be either of us taking the lead in greeting. As we became more familiar, he would ask on occasion, "Are you ready for the week?"

One day I must ask his name, I thought. In our tiny town, population barely 4,000, it was a wonder that we never crossed paths anywhere else: not in the grocery store, not at the post office, not at village events. But then I realized that I preferred the mystery of this gentle, soft-spoken dawn greeter to finding out who he was. I did ask him in passing one morning, after noticing for some time that my friend was no longer accompanied by the dog, where his dog was. He had to be put to sleep, he told me, the closest thing to personal information I ever learned about my early morning comrade.

Passing one another on these solitary walks began to mean something to me, though what exactly would have been difficult to capture in words. I looked for him in the gray light, in the drizzle, hunched against the wind; on balmy spring mornings I watched for him too. Though our paths did not always cross, his frequent appearance and his faithful greeting as we met had become a morning invocation. Here we were, fellow travelers who shared for a brief moment the expectation of a new day.

These unremarkable encounters with a nameless solitary have come to represent for me a consciousness of life's basic mystery; one tiny thread in a web of hidden patterns which give order and meaning to our lives. These threads pull into a matrix of complexity those strands of the ordinary, of the simplest things, of modest efforts, of unasked for and undeserved grace. Such consciousness offers a "sweet mysterious strength," which most of us glimpse, observes Thomas Gardner, only at extraordinary moments.

The truth is, we can bear only so much awareness as we go about our daily business. The Victorian writer George Eliot knew this, as reflected in her famous statement: "If we had a keen vision and feeling of all ordinary human life, it would be like hearing the grass grow and the squirrel's heart beat, and we should die of that roar which lies on the other side of silence. As it is, the quickest of us walk about well-wadded with stupidity." We teeter, as it were, on that edge of awareness that acknowledges some overall pattern of connection or that furnishes an inkling of life's hidden symmetry. All the while, we strive for balance and seek sensible paths.

It comes down, finally, to the time and space we occupy in the day-to-day: cultivating an awareness of the unexpected in the commonplace, noticing the interruptions, and welcoming the sudden turns which catch us by surprise. Acknowledging a connection with others requires a humble recognition that we need one another to awaken consciousness, and that some things are out of our hands. We have but to remind ourselves of the individuals who filter through our lives at certain forks and bends in the path to know this: prompters, conversation partners, strangers, comforters, and friends. Maggie and Cynthia were two such companions.

✛

Maggie and Cynthia

It was an April Monday, and I had just returned from another weekend on the road. I was still new in the presidency. As I often did walking to work, I began to pray. I should say I tried to pray, because I found that I could not still myself enough to frame the words. My thoughts made little sense as I tried to order and examine those tasks which would need immediate attention. Alongside the usual preoccupations of fund raising and capital projects, I knew we were at a critical stage in the dean search. I found myself dizzied by a sense of competing urgencies. I simply could not pray

In the chaos of that Monday, I did not have time to read all my e-mail. But when I logged on the next day, I found a note from Maggie: "One of the things that came to me as I was praying for you is that God will give you the gift of discernment as you are constantly faced with more than you can do." I was dumbfounded by both the timing and the message. Here again God was getting personal, it seemed. It was a humbling and awesome lesson, a reminder that when I could not pray for myself there was someone there to carry me along.

Maggie and I had developed an unlikely friendship since she lived in another state and was housebound because of health limitations. This acquaintance had sprung out of a chance phone conversation a few months before when I had called to speak with her husband, a former Bluffton board member. At that point, Maggie and I had not met. Because her husband had served on the presidential search committee, she knew more about me than I did about her. However, in that telephone call I was drawn in immediately by this lively woman eager to talk and by the discovery that we were both avid readers. What my business was with her husband, who eventually came on the phone, has long been forgotten; but that first "meeting" with Maggie was to remain unforgettable. We would discover through correspondence that we could share freely the private quandaries and personal dilemmas we faced in the day-to-day, she in her physical confinement and me in a public role.

Unplanned, this long-distance friendship was to become important for each of us in cultivating openness to a deeper consciousness of God's work in and around us. If that steady flow of letters over a ten-year presidency sustained me in both the satisfactions and frustrations of daily work, there was another woman who, unbeknownst to either of us at the beginning, would prove a timely influence as I considered the question of a college presidency in the first place.

While still dean at Eastern Mennonite University, I had met Cynthia, a Christian Scientist from Washington, D.C., who would be moving to the community. Cynthia was an accomplished scholar, a deeply committed Christian, and an activist dedicated to the work of peace. When first introduced, I felt inexplicably that here was someone I needed to get to know.

We came from very different backgrounds and religious traditions, but our common search for understanding God's purposes drew us together. I usually worked at my desk over the noon hour but began to take time for regular lunches with Cynthia, either at her table or mine. Over soup and bread, quesadillas and fruit, or whatever was in the refrigerator, we carried on conversations about our work and responsibility to others. She already knew a lot about Mennonites and their peacebuilding efforts. I knew virtually nothing about Christian Scientists, so this was a time of sharing faith and expanding awareness.

Each of us was facing change—or about to face change. In Cynthia's case she was settling into an unfamiliar community; she was adjusting to the loss of city life. I could listen and encourage Cynthia as she plunged into her new assignment. I was at the point of a dawning premonition that my life was about to take a different direction. It was this friendship with a person from outside my sphere of acquaintances that provided a space in which to test the nudge that something new was afoot.

When the call came regarding the Bluffton presidency, Cynthia served as a sounding board and patient listener as I stewed around in fuzzy fear, worrying again about the public aspects of the role. There at Cynthia's kitchen table, she helped me clarify that this was more about the institution than it was about me: "All you need to do is to speak for the college. You only have to represent this wonderful place to others." It suddenly seemed so simple. I could do that, giving voice to a passion for education and a commitment to service.

Maggie and Cynthia: two women whose lives have taught me something about a buoyant approach to life. They have shown me that we need each other. And that—in the convergence of time, place, and people—we are found by one another even as God seeks us out. I should no longer be surprised when it happens, but I am, pondering the randomness of it all, yet knowing that it is more.

✠

The Mind's Life

The impulse instilled by the Creator to make connections, to seek and to find, to know and to understand, is expressed in relationships. But essential, life-giving connections also have been forged for me through a lifetime of reading. I wonder about the curious way certain books or biblical passages, particular poets, novelists, and philosophers find me precisely when I need them. One of the great joys of my life has been the astonishing discovery, at critical junctures of decision-making or in those murky realities in which we muddle around, of just the right words which speak to a personal need. I no longer have to be convinced that this is not coincidence or pure luck. I have this whimsical image of some great Puppeteer in charge of manuscripts ancient and modern who, with perfect timing, directs a particular message my way just when it is required.

To give attention to the mind's life is why I read. It is the way I make a connection between what is inside and what is going on around me. It is also the way I recognize what is going on in my mind. Thus reading has become a life-long habit, a way into and a way out of myself.

By reading, I have been able to give myself permission to speak, finding a way through the strictures of silence imposed on women in my growing up. There is a certain irony in the fact that because "Word" (the Bible) was given such a high place in every single aspect of church, family, and communal life, "word" in its myriad forms (novels, poetry, story, legend, commentary, history, biography, religious works) could not be discounted outright. Thus I continue to search out a path through words, both the Holy Word and the infinite variety of the rest.

Writing has become a companion to reading, another way to care for the mind's life. It becomes an exercise in figuring out what I think. The journal, particularly, has served as a way to examine, in privacy and solitude, the way God enters my life. It serves as a way to touch the center, to evoke the still point which makes living possible. I have come to recognize that writing may be, for me, the truest form of prayer.

At the same time, writing serves a practical purpose. The journal provides a workspace, a place to hammer out and turn over those daily matters that deserve a second thought. It serves as a record, lest they be lost, of those fleeting encounters that stop us in our tracks; of insights which appall or inspire as we seek to understand what it means to be human.

And finally I write to offer prayers of gratitude for the convergences and fortuities which conspire to reveal a plan and purpose designed not just for humankind but for each of God's children. It is a good place to be, as I am today, when I can say with increasing conviction, to borrow W. H. Auden's words, "I do not believe in Chance; I believe in Providence and Miracles." In my experience, that makes each day fraught with humbling possibilities, including an encounter with the sacred.

Notes

Author's Preface

"Living is a form of not being sure, not knowing what next or how" is attributed to the American dancer and choreographer, Agnes De Mille.

Czeslaw Milosz's observation is quoted by Kathleen Norris in *The Virgin of Bennington* (New York: Riverhead Books, 2001), 254.

W. S. Di Piero, "In the Flea Market of the Mind," *The New York Times Book Review*, March 8, 1998, 4. The entire quotation is this: "Remembering is an act of the imagination. Any account we make of our experiences is an exercise in reinventing the self. Even when we think we're accurately reporting past events, persons, objects, places, and their sequence, we're theatricalizing the self and its world." Di Piero's statement introduces his review of Luc Sante's *The Factory of Facts* (New York: Pantheon Books, 1998).

Part One: Place

As background for my early years as a part of the Oregon Mennonite community, I consulted Hope Lind's, *Apart and Together: Mennonites in Oregon and Neighboring States 1876-1976* (Scottdale, Pa.: Herald Press, 1990).

I am particularly drawn to the Oregon poet, William Stafford, whose quote is found in his *You Must Revise Your Life* (Ann Arbor: University of Michigan Press, 1986), 99-100. I first encountered this description of poetry via Kathleen Norris in *The Virgin of Bennington* (New York: Riverhead Books, 2001), 104.

Weaving "lies and lives together" in the recall of family anecdotes is Lynda Sexson's term. She offers particular insights into how memory functions in our lives. See Sexson's, *Ordinarily Sacred* (Charlottesville: University of Virginia Press, 1992).

Part Two: Fortuities

Of particular value in reconstructing the California years and in confirming many of my memories was an article "by one of the workers" about the Sacramento rescue mission: "Fourth Anniversary of a Great Work," *Missionary Evangel* 10, no. 3 (April, May, June 1958): 1, 15-16. The report includes four photos: a street view of the mission, a service in progress, a prayer room seeker and the "Sisters preparing food in the Mission kitchen."

It is a character in Marilynn Robinson's *Gilead* (New York: Farrar, Straus and Giroux, 2004) who speaks of visions "that come to us only in memory, in retrospect." See Thomas Gardner's review of *Gilead,* "This Poor Gray Ember of Creation," *Books and Culture,* March/April 2005: 15.

Kathleen Roberts Skerritt speaks of "fortuities" as "signs . . . given in time and through contingency, rich, potent, consequential, yet composed of stuff that is just crawling around on the ground." See *Context,* July 2004, B6-7.

Part Three: The Large Questions

Theodore Roethke, *The Norton Anthology of American Literature.* Vol. 2. (New York: W. W. Norton & Company, 1979), 2267, 2272.

See Joan Didion essay collections, particularly, *Slouching Towards Bethlehem* (New York: Simon and Schuster, 1968) and *The White Album* (New York: Simon and Schuster, 1979).

John Gardner, *On Moral Fiction* (New York: Basic Books, 1978), 100.

F. Scott Fitzgerald, "The Crack-Up," *The Fitzgerald Reader.* Ed. Arthur Mizener (New York: Charles Scribner's Sons, 1963), 405.

The interview with my eighty-five-year-old-grandfather, Frank Kropf, took place in 1972. Later the recording was transcribed by his daughter, Berniece Kropf Schmucker. A portion of that interview was published in *Mennonite Life,* June 1987, 11-12. A more extended version was included in "Memories of Mary: The Swiss Maid Who Became My Grandmother, and Many Other Family Memories," by Berniece Schmucker, 2000.

Sherri Hostetler, "Say Yes Quickly," In *A Cappella: Mennonite Voices in Poetry,* ed. Ann Hostetler (Iowa City, University of Iowa Press, 2003), 126. Reprinted by permission.

Part Four: Finding the Way

Weather modeling and the Butterfly Effect is treated extensively in James Gleick's fascinating book, *Chaos: Making a New Science* (New York: Viking, 1987).

The irreplaceable and essential nature of the "mundane" in our lives, as noted in my journal, is based on an observation by Kathleen Dean Moore in the Autumn 2004 issue of the *Oregon Quarterly*.

For more from Margaret J. Wheatley, see *Leadership and the New Science* (San Francisco: Berrett-Koehler Publishers, 1994), 150. Wheatley is quoting from Loren Eiseley in *The Star Thrower* (San Diego: Harvest/HBJ, 1978), 214, who references Ralph Waldo Emerson. Emerson's original statement appears in "Experience," *Selected Writings of Ralph Waldo Emerson* (New York: New American Library, 1965), 327.

It was Robertson Davis who said, "By an agency that is not coincidence . . . we find, and are found by, the books we need to enlarge and complete us." *The Merry Heart: Reflections on Reading, Writing, and the World of Books* (New York: Penguin Books, 1998), 26.

Part Five: Seasons of the Presidency

This section draws from my personal journal and acknowledges a whole constellation of writers who were my tutors in the joys and misgivings of the presidency.

For the researchers' comments on visionaries, see *Common Fire: Lives of Commitment in a Complex World*, by Laurent A. Parks, Cheryl H. Keen, James P. Keen, and Sharon Daloz Parks (Boston: Beacon Press, 1996), 205.

T.S. Eliot, "East Coker," *Four Quartets* (New York: Harcourt Brace Jovanovich, 1971).

For more on chosen ness and humility, see Henri J. M. Nouwen, *Life of the Beloved: Spiritual Living in a Secular World* (New York: Crossroad, 2004), 50, 97-98.

This is a contemporary rendering of Psalm 19:13 by Eugene H. Peterson in *The Message: New Testament with Psalms and Proverbs* (Colorado Springs, Col.: NavPress, 1993).

This bit of Flannery O'Connor wisdom is found in her last letter before her death from Lupus. See *The Habit of Being: Letters,* ed. Sally Fitzgerald (New York: Farrar, Straus, Giroux, 1988), 596.

Part Six: Life Work

"Healing," in *What Are People For? Essays by Wendell Berry* (San Francisco: North Point Press, 1990), 12.

Donald Hall, *Life Work* (Boston: Beacon Press, 1993), 23.

Kathleen Norris, *Amazing Grace: A Vocabulary of Faith* (New York: Riverhead Books, 1998), 14.

Donald Hall relates the Henry Moore anecdote in *The Old Life* (Boston: Houghton Mifflin Company, 1996), 70.

Margaret J. Wheatley autograph in personal copy of *Finding Our Way:*

Leadership for an Uncertain Time (San Francisco: Berrett-Koehler Publishers, 2005).

Linda Hill discusses these leadership principles in "Leadership Development, *Futures Forum 2005*.

Bluffton University professor Dr. Karen Klassen Harder must be credited with this concise description of the leader's responsibility to listen, learn, support and respect.

Rosabeth Moss Kanter, an expert on organizational change, writes insightfully about leadership and the work place in *Confidence: How Winning Streaks and Losing Streaks Begin and End* (New York: Crown Business, 2004).

Wendell Berry has a collection of poems entitled *The Country of Marriage* (San Diego: A Harvest Book, Harcourt Brace & Company, 1973) which is only peripherally about marriage, but the term nevertheless is a wonderful descriptor.

Epilogue

This term "sweet mysterious strength" is Thomas Gardner's, who uses it in a somewhat different context in "This Poor Gray Ember of Creation," *Books and Culture* (March/April 2005), 15.

George Eliot, *Middlemarch: An Authoritative Text, Backgrounds, Reviews and Criticism*, ed Bert G. Hornback. (New York: W. W. Norton & Company, 1977), 135.

W. H. Auden, "Introduction: Concerning the Unpredictable," *The Star Thrower* by Loren Eiseley (San Diego: Harvest, 1978), 17.

Credits

Portions of *At Powerline and Diamond Hill* are indebted to the previously published sources by Lee Snyder listed below.

1. "An Interview with Frank Kropf," ed. Berniece Kropf Schmucker, in *Mennonite Life* 42, II (June 1987): 11-12.

2. "Red Poppies," in *She Has Done a Good Thing: Mennonite Women Leaders Tell Their Stories,* ed. Mary Swartley and Rhoda Keener (Scottdale, Pa.: Herald Press, 1999), 247-255.

3. "The Mystery of the Living Word," in *Telling Our Stories: Personal Accounts of Engagement with Scripture,* ed. Ray Gingerich and Earl Zimmerman (Telford, Pa.: Cascadia Publishing House, 2006), 189-197.

4. "The Testament God Gave Back," *DreamSeeker Magazine,* August 2007, 16-17.

5. "Fortuities and Convergences," in *Continuing the Journey: The Geography of Our Faith,* ACRS Memoirs vol. 2, ed. Nancy V. Lee (Telford, Pa.: Cascadia Publishing House, 2009), 7-25.

Brief portions of these Bible versions are included in the book:
Part III, Romans 8:28—King James Version; Psalm 139 passages—New International Version (NIV)
Part V, Deuteronomy 30:11, 14—NIV; Psalm 19:13—*The Message*
Part VI, John 15:16—NIV

Acknowledgments

I am grateful to family members who assisted me in reconstructing the early years in the Harrisburg community and in our family's move to California. A few written records related to the church and to the Kropf family were useful and contributed significantly to the piecing together of my own story. Berniece Kropf Schmucker, my father's sister, graciously responded to questions as I attempted to clarify early memories. I also drew on Berniece's compilation of family stories in *Memories of Mary: The Swiss Maid Who Became My Grandmother and Many Other Family Memories* (2000).

Conversations with my mother, Ruth Elizabeth Stewart Kropf, supplemented my own recollections of childhood. Also, my father's "Memories," published posthumously in *Memories of Mary,* provided additional detail. Another background source was *Daniel J. Kropf and Anna Hostetler and Descendants Family Record: 1861-1985,* n.d., with this notation: "This book was made with love for all generations of the Daniel J. Kropf Family. Assembled by Arzalea (Kropf) Hostetler, Arlene (Smucker) Hostetler, Merle Kropf." This booklet was given to me by my mother and father in 1985. The genealogies and birth records supplemented by short "life histories" of my grandfather and his siblings furnished invaluable background information. I was delighted also to find old documents related to the Harrisburg Mennonite Church, which included "Family Lines" (charter members 1911, family tree of charter members, and family tree of deaf membership); a chronology of church leaders and a history of the church building.

Any factual errors are of course my own, but I must thank all those who added immeasurably to this process of remembering by sharing their own stories of early family and church life.

A word of appreciation to Paul Weaver, reference librarian at Bluffton University, who helped me track down several elusive references and to Michael A. King, Cascadia Publishing House LLC, who provided encouragement along the way. Finally to Del, who read carefully and offered gentle counsel, my immeasurable gratitude.

The Author

Credit: Ray C. Gingerich

Born on a farm in Oregon and raised in a Mennonite community, Lee Snyder's life and work follows a trajectory that she herself would never have imagined. She, her husband Del, and two preschool daughters lived in West Africa in the late 1960s, stationed at the Qua Ibo Secondary School in the heart of the equatorial rain forest. Only after returning from Nigeria, when her daughters entered elementary school, was Lee able to complete college.

The family's move in the early 1970s from the West Coast to Virginia for her husband's appointment to the mathematics department at Eastern Mennonite University (EMU) led to Lee's graduate work in English literature, teaching, and eventual appointment as vice-president and academic dean, EMU. Following twelve years as dean, Lee accepted the presidency at Bluffton (Oh.) University. As eighth president of the institution, and its first female head, Lee served at Bluffton ten years.

Moving back to Virginia after officially retiring from the Bluffton presidency in 2006, Lee continues a variety of assignments with educational organizations, boards of trustees, and the church. She and her husband divide their time between Virginia and Oregon where they maintain a residence. Lee and Del are members of Community Mennonite Church, Harrisonburg, Virginia, and associate members of Salem Mennonite Church in Oregon.

LaVergne, TN USA
15 December 2010
208977LV00002B/49/P